The Navy War
An Oral and Visual History of World War II at Sea

The Navy War
An Oral and Visual History of World War II at Sea

Arthur B. Layton, Jr.

With photographs from the National Archives
and the Department of the Navy

Castine, Maine

**The Navy War:
An Oral and Visual History
of World War II at Sea**

©
1992
by Arthur B. Layton, Jr.

All rights reserved

Published by Country Roads Press
P.O. Box 286, Lower Main Street
Castine, Maine 04421

Designed by Pedro A. Noa

ISBN 0-9630646-9-x

Library of Congress Catalog Card No. 91-077858

Printed in the United States of America

10 9 8 7 6 5 4 3 2 1

Contents

Introduction	vii
Chapter One	PEARL HARBOR: Out of the Rising Sun **3**
Chapter Two	MIDWAY: Silent Subs and Fast Carriers **21**
Chapter Three	GUADALCANAL: Terror in the Night **39**
Chapter Four	NORTH ATLANTIC: The U-boat War **53**
Chapter Five	SILENT AND DEEP: The Submarine War in the Pacific **67**
Chapter Six	NORMANDY: A Bridge to Victory **83**
Chapter Seven	LEYTE GULF: The Fight for the Philippines **99**
Chapter Eight	OKINAWA: Hell Fighters **109**
Chapter Nine	GOING HOME: Back in the U.S. of A. **121**

Introduction

Anyone who was old enough at the time to listen to a radio invariably remembers where they were and what they were doing on December 7, 1941. News of the unprovoked and devastating Japanese attack on Pearl Harbor transformed and unified the nation as nothing had before. With an explosive shock—like a torpedo slamming into the hull of a warship—the nation came of age that day. The complacency of isolationism was no longer possible. Suddenly the United States of America was a citizen—perhaps the most important citizen—of a world on the brink of utter chaos. It was a very heavy responsibility indeed.

The weight of that responsibility fell most heavily on the U.S. Navy. The first disastrous battle had already made it all too clear that, initially at least, the Navy would do most of the fighting. It is easy to imagine sailors and admirals alike turning to their comrades and saying, "Looks like we've got ourselves a Navy war."

It was true. Overnight, sailors became the tallest men in America. The great watery expanses of the Atlantic had once seemed a barrier against invasion. But now, with the Navy's once-mighty battleship fleet in smoking ruins at Pearl Harbor, the oceans offered little protection. They had become wide-open highways inviting attack. All that stood between the enemy and the beaches of California or North Carolina were the Navy's battered hardware and the fighting spirit of its men.

Whether deck officer with a college education or seaman "deuce" without a high school diploma, each sailor faced the task of stopping the enemy and winning the war with his own personal mixture of excitement, dread, and determination. And each man who survived the conflict came home with indelible memories. Now, after more than fifty years on the ordinary oceans of everyday life, the sailors who fought the Battle of the Atlantic, struggled at Midway or Okinawa, or saw action off the shores of Europe or North Africa still recall those extraordinary experiences with near-perfect clarity.

In the pages of this book, you'll meet a number of those sailors and read their personal stories. Authentic combat photographs from the Navy Department and the National Archives help them recapture the drama of the war's most decisive sea battles. Come aboard with them now as they relate the exciting and unforgettable history of the Navy War.

The Navy War
An Oral and Visual History
of World War II at Sea

Chapter One

PEARL HARBOR:
Out of the Rising Sun

Destroyer USS *Shaw* explodes at Pearl Harbor.

Two hundred nautical miles north of its target, the Japanese Imperial Navy's Strike Force rode to heavy seas kicked up by a 20-knot breeze. An hour and 45 minutes earlier, at 6:00 A.M., Admiral Chuichi Nagumo had ordered the first assault wave of 183 warplanes into the air. One after the other they roared down the decks of their carriers, the *Hiryu, Soryu, Akagi, Kaga, Shokaku*, and *Zuikaku*, hurried along into the darkness by cries of "Banzai! Banzai!"

Admiral Nagumo had already accomplished a tactical maneuver unparalleled in the history of naval warfare. Without detection, he had brought his massive fleet halfway across the Pacific, some 3,500 nautical miles, and positioned it perfectly for a surprise attack on the key United States naval base at Pearl Harbor. Now Nagumo waited patiently for a message from his young fliers. Would their attack be successful? Had they caught the Americans unaware? In a few minutes he would know.

The success of the attack—and its disastrous results—had been foreseen a full sixteen years earlier. With uncanny accuracy, British naval journalist Hector C. Bywater had predicted the bombing of Pearl Harbor in his book *The Great Pacific War*, published during the 1920s. But American and British military commanders had not needed to read Bywater's book to realize that an attack was coming. Their intelligence services had already alerted them. What they did not know was *where* the Japanese would strike. Hawaii, Sydney, and Singapore all stood high on the guess list, and Singapore seemed the most likely target.

Tora! Tora! Tora!

Flying at 9,750 feet above the water, with heavy cloud cover down to 4,875 feet, Mitsuo Fuchida hoped the Americans had guessed wrong. Fuchida was commander of the first wave, and just now he was peering down into the clouds hoping to catch sight of his target. Suddenly the clouds parted, allowing Fuchida a glimpse of waves breaking in long white streaks onto the beaches of Oahu Island. It was 7:49 A.M., and over his shoulder Fuchida could see the sun rising. He told his radioman to order the attack.

Responding instantly to Fuchida's order, Lieutenant Commander Shigeru Murata's torpedo planes began their descent, and Lieutenant Commander Kakuichi Takahadi's dive bombers started to climb. Fuchida's own high-level bombers angled for Barbers Point while Lieutenant Commander Shigira Itaya's fighters raced onward to sweep the sky of American fighters. (Only four U.S. fighters would get into the air that day. Outnumbered hundreds to one, all would be shot down.)

Seconds ticked by. The world held its breath.

Pearl Harbor and Ford Island as they appeared to Japanese pilots at the start of their daring raid on the morning of December 7, 1941. At the center and right of this Imperial Navy photograph (captured later in the war) can be seen the outlines of two enemy bombers carrying out low-level attacks. Near the center of the picture, a plume of water shoots skyward as a torpedo strikes the stern of a battleship. The Japanese later described the performance of their pilots during the attack as "reminiscent of the gods."

Torpedo planes had already made a mess of once-proud Battleship Row when a Japanese pilot snapped this picture just as dive bombers were about to renew the attack. The ships shown here are (left to right) *Nevada, Arizona* and *Vestal, Tennessee* and *West Virginia, Maryland* and *Oklahoma*. Notice the large slicks formed by oil gushing from ruptured fuel tanks.

Commander Fuchida also may have held his breath as he rapidly assessed the situation below. He saw no American fighters rising to meet him, no flashes from antiaircraft batteries on the ground. Lined up two-by-two, the great battleships of the United States Pacific Fleet lay motionless and unprotected. At 7:53 A.M., only four minutes after giving the order to attack, Fuchida told his radioman to send a message to the Japanese fleet.

"Tora! Tora! Tora!" Those were the words Admiral Nagumo was waiting to hear. Their literal translation was "Tiger! Tiger! Tiger!" but to Nagumo they had a different meaning altogether. They were a coded signal telling him that American forces on Oahu had been caught completely by surprise. Facing limited resistance, his pilots would surely strike the American fleet a heavy blow. Nagumo ordered a second attack wave into the air. It was now clear that he and his men would accomplish their mission, but Nagumo wasted little time on self-congratulation. Better than most of his fellow officers, Nagumo understood that the war had now entered a new, highly unpredictable and dangerous phase for the Imperial Navy, one that could have dire consequences for Japan.

The morning's events were already having dire consequences for the servicemen and residents of Oahu. As the first wave of bombers swooped down, church bells were ringing, morning papers were being delivered, and sailors were readying themselves for their daily shipboard routines. This being Sunday, many servicemen were still asleep. They had gone to bed in the service of a nation at peace—technically, at least—but they were about to be rudely awakened to the harsh realities of World War II. Lieutenant Commander Takahadi's dive bombers opened the attack by hitting, in rapid succession, Wheeler Field, Hickham Field, and the Navy bases on Ford Island in the center of Pearl Harbor. By 8:00 A.M., Lieutenant Commander Itaya's fighters had secured complete air superiority, and using incendiary bullets to set fuel tanks on fire, began strafing the airfields which were still reeling from the dive bomber attack. Then Commander Fuchida's high-level bombers started their assault on Battleship Row just as ship and shore batteries opened up, smudging the sky dark gray with antiaircraft bursts. The cloud cover had caused the bombers to miss their release point, and they had to circle at least three times before zeroing in on their targets.

Smoldering wreck of the *Arizona*. An armor-piercing bomb struck the magazine, and the battleship blew up killing more than 1,100 sailors.

A motor launch rescues a sailor from the water near the burning battleships *West Virginia* and *Tennessee*. During their devastating raid, the Japanese sank or seriously damaged six battleships along with dozens of other vessels. They also destroyed scores of warplanes, mostly on the ground. By the time the attack was over, the U.S. Navy's Pacific strength had been cut in half.

A stroke of luck may have saved the U.S. from defeat in the Pacific. By sheer coincidence, no American aircraft carriers were in Pearl Harbor at the time of the attack. Shown here as they appeared in 1938, several years before the war, are the carriers (top to bottom) *Ranger, Lexington,* and *Saratoga.* Note the antiquated biplanes crowding the deck of the *Saratoga*.

President Franklin Delano Roosevelt described December 7, 1941, as "a day that will live in infamy." Here he signs the declaration of war against Japan.

Chapter One • PEARL HARBOR

Three days after the attack on Pearl Harbor, Japan's German and Italian allies declared war on the United States. Hitler and Mussolini ride triumphantly through the streets of Munich.

But the torpedo plane pilots had the most difficult job. Equipped with special shallow-water torpedos designed for release at 66 feet above the water, Lieutenant Commander Murata's torpedo planes concentrated on the eight U.S. battleships tied to quays beside Ford Island. Since their altimeters would not work at such low altitudes, they had to estimate the correct drop height as well as drop speed and range while flying at reduced speed through enemy fire. Then, having dropped their loads, they had to veer off sharply to avoid crashing into their targets.

A Navy War

With their attention fixed on the battleships, few of the Japanese torpedo pilots likely gave much thought to the white-uniformed sailors firing at them with World War I rifles from the submarine base in Southeast Loch. Among them was Seaman Second Class William "Mac" McKinley, who, just minutes before the attack, had been standing with his mates in a Sunday morning formation. Now they were fighting for their lives. Some did not recognize the attacking planes as Japanese. But they all knew they were in a war—a Navy war—even if they were not that sure who they were fighting.

At 8:54 A.M., almost exactly an hour after the first attack, a second wave of 170 bombers and torpedo planes hit the island. By the time they had finished their bombing and strafing, the U.S. Pacific Fleet had taken a severe beating. Proud Pearl Harbor was a shambles, and several of the Navy's biggest and finest battleships lay in smoking ruins. More than 2,000 U.S. Navy officers and men were killed—many of them when the battleship *Arizona* exploded—and 710 were wounded during the air strike. The number of killed and wounded was three times that of the Navy's *combined losses in the Spanish-American War* and World War I. Army and Marine Corps losses totaled 327 killed and 433 wounded. Seventy civilians were killed, most of them government employees who worked at military airfields. Others died when stray antiaircraft shells exploded in the streets of Honolulu.

By comparison, Japanese losses were light. They lost a total of only 55 officers and men, the crews of the nine fighters, fifteen dive bombers, and five torpedo planes that were either shot down or crashed into the sea. By 1:00 P.M. all of the Japanese planes that were coming back were safely aboard the six carriers. Then the strike force, which in addition to the carriers included two battleships, two heavy cruisers, one light cruiser, eleven destroyers, three submarines, and eight tankers, slipped away into the trackless Pacific.

By the time the U.S. joined the fighting, the war had already set much of the world on fire. German incendiary bombs torched this building in Sheffield near London.

Before America entered the war, the British stood virtually alone against the might of the Axis for more than a year. A mass raid by Germany's Luftwaffe throws billows of smoke and ash into the sky behind London's Tower Bridge.

A Waking Giant

While tactically brilliant, the bold Japanese surprise attack was not the decisive victory its planners had sought. The biggest disappointment for Japanese strategists was the fact that they had missed their most important targets. By sheer coincidence, the U.S. fleet carriers *Enterprise, Lexington,* and *Saratoga* were not in Pearl Harbor on December 7. When the bombers struck, *Saratoga* was in California for routine maintenance and repair. *Lexington* had just delivered scout bombers to Midway Island and *Enterprise* had just delivered Marine Corps fighter planes to Wake Island and was headed back to Pearl Harbor. In fact, she was only a few hundred miles out of Honolulu when the electrifying news of the attack reached her commander, Rear Admiral William Halsey.

Psychologically, the attack had an effect exactly the opposite of what Japanese planners had hoped for and expected. They had assumed their lightning victory at Pearl would demoralize the American public. Instead, it shook Americans out of their pervasive isolationism, uniting them behind an all-out war effort. Adding to the anger of Americans was the perception that the bombing was a "sneak attack." Japan's ambassador in Washington had been instructed to deliver his nation's declaration of war exactly 30 minutes before the attack. For

Caught in a worldwide, two-ocean war, the nation called on its entire military-aged population to "man the guns." By war's end, more than 15 million Americans had served in uniform.

In this war—for the first time in American history—large numbers of women as well as men answered the call to colors.

rather mundane reasons—among them a slow typist—the ambassador was late, and bombs were already falling on Pearl Harbor by the time he reached the U.S. State Department with the tardy declaration. The timing might seem trivial when compared to the impact of a torpedo on the hull of a battleship, but it was considered a point of honor both in the United States and Japan. Some Japanese now feared their country had "awakened a sleeping giant" and filled him with a "terrible resolve."

Giants draw their power from myth; ordinary people draw their strength from many sources. That is fortunate because it was not a giant, but ordinary American service men and women and their folks back home who would have to fight and win the war for the U.S. One such American was Seaman McKinley from Venice, California. He was eighteen and had been growing increasingly impatient with life in the Navy.

When he had signed up the year before, the Navy had held a natural attraction for McKinley. He had graduated at age seventeen from Venice High School right into the Great Depression. Being poor, "really poor," McKinley could not find a job that would support him and going to college or university was financially out of the question. His parents would have allowed him to stay at home, but the Navy's "See the World" bravado appealed to his yearning for adventure. His father had whetted his appetite for travel and adventure with tales of his own wanderings as a young man. Among other things, the elder McKinley had knocked around South Africa during the Boer War, joined a corps of irregulars led by British officers, and been captured by the Boers. Young Mac McKinley had heard these and other exciting stories while growing up, so in the Navy he looked for both opportunity and adventure. Until the morning of December 7, 1941, however, the Navy had shown him little of either.

Earlier in that year, after completing boot camp at San Diego, he had been assigned to the battleship *Nevada*. On the *Nevada*, he served as a Deck Force Seaman, First Division—"the lowest form of life on the planet," as McKinley describes it. "The living conditions were miserable. You slept in canvas hammocks and you lived out of a sea bag. There was a three-inch mattress and a pillow in the hammock. You washed clothes in a bucket, and you were allowed only one bucket of fresh water a day.

"They picked the meanest people they could find as masters-at-arms. These men would get up before reveille and stand nearby with night sticks. At the first sound of the bugle they would whack the nearest guy on the backside with the stick.

"Dungarees were not issued to seamen second class. We holystoned decks, swabbed out compartments, and polished brass in white uniforms which we cleaned daily in our buckets using salt water and saltwater soap. A lot of the jobs were make-work jobs—paint chipping or cleaning spittoons and heads.

"The *Nevada* had flush-type heads for officers and chief petty officers, but the rest of us had to use stainless steel troughs with water coming in one end and going out the other. There was a tray with removable seats over the trough. The water pressure was insufficient to force out everything, so we had to use pushers to get it going. Sometimes for entertainment we would take a large wad of toilet paper, light it, and let the water carry it down the trough. The flames and smoke would make people jump up from the seats as it passed along.

"The showers were open for one hour a day for most of us, which was totally inadequate for the number of people who had to use them. The compartment was so hot it was like going into a Turkish bath. There was an inspection every Saturday. The least spot on a uniform or your shoes meant no liberty. We learned to lay our uniforms flat between the mattress and the hammock to get most of the wrinkles out and then iron the rest.

"But the food was fair. It was certainly adequate, and we had enough to *eat*. Saturday mornings we always had baked beans, corn bread, and scrambled eggs. Sunday night was cold cuts."

McKinley's battle station was atop the mainmast in a gun tub which had two .50 caliber machine guns. He and the other members of the gun crews liked the bird bath, as they called it. It soared high above the rest of the ship, away from the crowd. But McKinley never got to fire the guns. At night he stood messenger watch or lifeboat watch, and he found little excitement in either task. He wanted to learn to launch a lifeboat, but his ship did not practice launches at night. He wanted to learn to steer the ship, but that was not allowed him either.

If life aboard *Nevada* was unfulfilling for an ambitious seaman second class, so was life ashore. It was a different Hawaii then. "The fleet was too big for

Sometimes the rich and famous also served in uniform. This photograph taken in 1942 shows movie idol and Lieutenant (j.g.) Douglas Fairbanks, Jr., standing watch with a fellow officer aboard the carrier *Wasp*.

Military life came as a shock to many Americans. For millions morning now began with the sharp, insistent call of reveille.

Honolulu. It just couldn't handle the traffic. The result was a lot of unpleasantness. Our opportunities for recreation were limited. We were allowed one liberty every three days in port. We were off at 1600 [4:00 P.M.] and had to be back by 1900 [7:00 P.M.]. We had to take boats ashore, and priority was given to officers, petty officers, leading seamen, rated seamen, and then us. Seamen 'deuces' were at the lowest end of the pecking order in the spit-and-polish prewar Navy. So we had to wait around for a boat to make several trips before it was our turn. You were lucky if you got ashore in an hour and now it's 1700 [5:00 P.M.], almost time to line up for the return trip.

"At first the only transport into Honolulu was taxis. So there would be a few thousand white hats waiting for five taxis, and this consumed more time. On the way back it was the same fight in reverse. Most of us didn't even bother going ashore on weekdays, but on weekends you could get off at noon and come back at 1900. So I didn't get to see a whole lot of Honolulu or Waikiki or anything else. I requested leave to go see some of the other islands, to see something besides Oahu, but it was never granted."

McKinley developed a considerable distaste for battleships. "It was not just that they were so restrictive, but the fact that you were held in such low regard. Some of the boatswains mates were real old-timers. Very strict and tough. They considered me and the other deuces pretty low-caliber people, or so I thought."

Crowded berths aboard a battleship.

So McKinley looked for a way to move up from the bottom. "The Navy had fleet schools where you could learn to be a gunner's mate or learn other jobs that led to being a rated man. I didn't care what school I went to. I just hoped it would lead to some kind of career, some kind of job." Unfortunately for McKinley, fleet school had its own drudgeries. "It turned out that for every certain number of people they put in fleet school, they had to send a man to clean compartments." When the Japanese hit Pearl Harbor, McKinley was the compartment cleaner for the fleet school at the Southeast Loch submarine base.

Chapter One • PEARL HARBOR

Seamen second class ("deuces") muscle their way through one of the grimiest and least desirable shipboard tasks, that of holystoning a deck.

"We were assembled waiting for the Star-Spangled Banner to be played. I looked off to the right and saw a bunch of planes diving on Ford Island. U.S. Navy planes used to make mock raids on Ford Island and other parts of Pearl Harbor. The usual route was to come out of clouds which were almost always there back of Pearl Harbor and make for Battleship Row. That was what these planes were doing.

"But then there was an explosion. My first thought was that some pilot couldn't pull out of his dive. There was another explosion. Was the whole squadron going to follow that guy in? I wondered if the Navy had found a way of making this [the fake bombing runs] more realistic. Then I remembered that they never had practice raids on Sunday. This was Sunday. So I thought... maybe...these are...Jap planes. Since I was just a little tyke, my father had said someday we were going to go to war with Japan. He didn't have connections in high places, but he read newspapers. We seamen deuces used to sit around discussing the possibility of a Japanese raid on Pearl Harbor. We always came to the conclusion that the Japanese couldn't get within a thousand miles of Pearl without our finding out about it.

Waiting to watch a movie below decks on a battleship.

"We were still lined up in formation, but a bunch of us decided we had to do something. We didn't have assigned battle stations, so we made our own. We ran down to the finger piers and broke into an armory. There we took World War I bolt-action Springfield rifles, and we took bandoliers of ammunition. We tied the bandoliers around our waists and across our chests and went out onto the finger piers to do battle. Anything that came within sight we shot at. I had never fired anything bigger than a .22, and these were .30 calibers."

The makeshift antiaircraft platoon started firing at the low-flying torpedo planes. McKinley was still not sure he was fighting the Japanese. "They had to come in low and came in quite close to us. I thought I could see the oriental eyes of the pilots. The tails of their planes had meatballs [the Japanese rising sun emblem] on them, but a lot of our planes used to have squadron insignias that looked similar. The bomb bays of U.S. torpedo planes concealed the torpedos. With Japanese planes you could see them. As the planes passed by and we fired at them, we could see the torpedos angling out.

"By one of the finger piers was the *Tautog*, an old World War I four-stacker destroyer. She was tied up with the stern out which meant the stern gun could fire at the torpedo planes as they went by on their way to Battleship Row. As the planes passed by, the four-stacker fired point-blank at them. One of the planes was hit and turned 90 degrees up so that you could see the meatballs on the wings. Up to that point I had been 90.7 percent sure we were at war with Japan. Now, I was 100 percent sure. The plane hit the water, and I believe it sank. We all yelled like we were at a football game when a plane we were shooting at began to smoke or went down.

"The Japs would swing around and strafe after finishing a bombing run. There was a lot of strafing. Also, there was quite a rain of bomb fragments and shrapnel around us from antiaircraft guns. We took positions on top of the barracks [and kept firing]. I wasn't scared, but I was really angry. I was so mad I didn't have room for any other emotion. I was half hoping they would come back. No, I really wasn't scared. That came later. Later in the war there were times of sheer terror."

Chapter Two

MIDWAY: Silent Subs and Fast Carrier

With smoke still rising from the wrecks of the once-mighty warships on Battleship Row, American commanders began to assess the dire military emergency confronting them. The surface fleet had been crippled by the heavy blow the Japanese had landed at Pearl Harbor. Along with the perilously exposed Hawaiian Islands, California and the entire U.S. West Coast lay under the threat of a large-scale Japanese assault. To hold back the enemy, Navy strategists fell back on those vessels with the lowest profile in the U.S. fleet—submarines. Cruising on the surface at night and submerged during the day, the subs fanned out in a broad arc to form a protective shield against the Japanese.

Fortunately, the Japanese bombers had ignored the submarine base at Pearl. It was no coincidence that Admiral Chester W. Nimitz formally took command of the Pacific Fleet on the deck of the USS *Grayling*, a submarine. Nimitz was a former submariner himself, and besides, the *Grayling* was the only appropriate vessel left in the harbor. With the exception of the carriers, which were at sea, much of the Pearl Harbor fleet had either been sunk or was on the West Coast for repairs.

America's submarines had been thrust suddenly into the watery front lines of the war and along with them Seaman (now Third Class) William McKinley. The bombs had hardly stopped falling when McKinley, who had seen firsthand what a torpedo could do, entered torpedo school at Pearl Harbor. But McKinley's

A call to general quarters scrambles pilots and sailors on an American flattop

ambitions were certainly not limited to torpedos. He also took a special entrance examination for admission to the United States Naval Academy in Annapolis, Maryland. It seemed a long shot, and he knew it would be a long time before he heard the results, but he thought it was worth a try. Just as he was graduating from torpedo school—at the top of his class—the USS *Nautilus* docked in Pearl Harbor. The *Nautilus* needed a crewman, and newly-minted Torpedoman Third Class McKinley got the job.

The assignment delighted the young sailor. The camaraderie and esprit de corps in the submarine service was rivaled only by that of carrier pilots. Unlike his experience on the *Nevada,* where he felt stuck on the lower rungs of the Navy ladder, McKinley now found himself in an elite group. Submarine sailors depended on one another and respected one another. On the *Nevada* he had wanted to learn and was rarely given the chance. Now he was actually required to learn much of what there was to know about the *Nautilus*. Whatever their jobs, every sailor had to learn every valve and lever on the submarine. Everyone else's life depended on it.

His first night aboard, McKinley was given a .45 caliber automatic pistol (he had never fired one), a cartridge belt, a telescope, and a logbook, and was

Although its battleship fleet had been blasted at Pearl Harbor, the U.S. Navy still had its fleet carriers. A flight of Navy war birds patrol the skies above the *Enterprise* while an escort destroyer trails.

Chapter Two • MIDWAY

put on the gangway watch. He considered it a job equivalent to that of officer of the deck on a battleship. The fresh responsiblity made him plenty nervous, but the watch passed without incident. McKinley filled in the log, but he missed the section on weather. When the executive officer pointed out the omission the next day, the young sailor was mortified. Would they boot him off the sub? The executive officer suggested completing the weather section with figures averaged out from previous entries, and the two submariners filled in the log together.

As the new man on board McKinley needed to learn all he could as quickly as he could because the *Nautilus* was about to be ordered into battle. With a fresh load of torpedos, the submarine left Pearl Harbor and headed west northwest, its destination Midway Atoll, 1,136 nautical miles from Honolulu. McKinley didn't know it at the time, but he and his shipmates were about to take on one of the

A formation of U.S. Navy Avengers.

largest and most powerful Japanese fleets ever assembled—-almost the entire strength of the Japanese Imperial Navy.

Once underway, the captain described the situation to the crew. He told them they were headed for a major action. He told them they must be ready to unleash as much havoc as possible on the Japanese. But neither the captain nor his crew could have known they were about to participate in one of history's most significant battles. In fact, the dramatic events of the next few days would prove to be the turning point of the war in the Pacific.

During the voyage, McKinley was ordered to take the wheel, something he had often wanted to do, but had never done before. The officer of the deck had told him to sound the alarm bell when he heard the command to dive. So when

Except for the outnumbered U.S. carrier fleet, only a thin picket line of submarines held the Japanese back from the American west coast during the early months of the war. A poster tells the submarine story as Navy recruiters saw it.

the captain turned and told the officer of the deck to "take her down," McKinley immediately hit the alarm bell. "Not now!" shouted the captain. "We have three men up there!"

But it was too late to stop the dive. As soon as the bell sounded, the crew started spinning valves and pulling levers with well practiced precision. When they heard the alarm and felt the submarine begin its dive, the three men on deck wasted no time. They shot down the ladder so fast it appeared to McKinley that the first sailor was carrying the other two on his shoulders.

The eager torpedoman had unintentionally become an innovator. To make diving faster, the *Nautilus* scrapped the standard procedure of clearing the deck watch before sounding the alarm. Later, the word was passed to the rest of the submarine fleet, and eventually McKinley's error would become a standard dive practice. But there was no time to consider new procedures just now. Somewhere to the northwest lay a Japanese battle fleet—a big one.

Riding on a Tide of Victory

The warships of the Imperial Navy were riding on a tide of victory as they sailed toward tiny Midway with its isolated American garrison. Japanese forces had never been more confident for in China, the Philippines, Indo-China, and the South Pacific they were meeting with success after success. The Japanese command saw Midway as one more sandy island step on the watery road to conquest of the Pacific basin.

The fleet weighed anchor off the island of Hashirajima, south of Hiroshima, on Japan's Navy Day, May 27, 1942. The date was an auspicious one since it marked the anniversary of Japan's destruction of the Russian Navy thirty-seven years before at the Battle of Tsushima. That victory, like the one at Pearl Harbor, had been achieved through surprise. Now the Japanese admiralty expected to spring yet another overwhelming surprise attack at Midway. They believed that once they had seized the island, the U.S. Navy would be forced to commit its best aircraft carriers in an all-out counterattack. When the American carriers appeared, Japanese bombers and torpedo planes would be waiting for them. That was the plan.

The Japanese had laid the plan with their characteristic eye for meticulous detail. In March, they began a thorough reconnaissance of the approaches to Midway and the Aleutians. The Japanese had plenty of submarines, and now they pressed them into service keeping track of the American fleet. Where were the remaining battleships? And above all, where were the carriers? Meanwhile, to keep the Americans guessing, they carefully screened the movements of their own fleet. Using submarines to refuel flying boats at French Frigate Shoals, about 500 miles northwest of Hawaii, Imperial Navy pilots overflew Oahu at night, dropping a few stray bombs to confuse U.S. strategists.

The decision to take Midway as an advance base for air patrols was arrived at only after months of painstaking strategic analysis. Admiral Isoroku Yamamoto and other members of the Naval General Staff in Tokyo realized the

The submarine *Trout* delivers a shipment of gold to Honolulu. The bullion was evacuated from the fortress on Corregidor in the Philippines to keep it from falling into enemy hands.

operation would overextend Japanese fleet operations. But the likely benefits outweighed the risk. To fuel its industrial complex and assure the continued success of its military, Japan aimed to grab the abundant oil supplies available in Southeast Asia. To that end it had been pummeling American, British, Dutch, and Australian forces standing between them and the oil. But Japanese leaders had even more ambitious long-range goals—to secure their hold on the Pacific by taking Hawaii to the east, establishing air superiority over the Indian Ocean to the west, and eventually linking up with German and Italian forces in the Near East.

It was a tall order. The oil-rich Dutch East Indies (now Indonesia) had been taken, but the Dutch navy was still shooting back whenever it could. The British were still in the fight despite the fall of Singapore. The tiny Australian navy was throwing punches whenever it could to keep its country from being isolated. And

On its way to bomb Japan, an Army B-25 roars off the deck of the USS *Hornet*. The Doolittle Raid on Tokyo, April 18, 1942, did little damage but wounded Japanese pride.

the United States Navy, which had received more than a bloody nose at Pearl Harbor, was becoming bolder and more aggressive every day. In February, American aircraft carrier task forces had attacked the Marshall Islands, Rabaul, Wake, Marcus Island, and eastern New Guinea. The U.S. fleet would have to be hit again, and hard, if Japan was to secure the resources of Southeast Asia. The Japanese bombers and torpedo planes that blasted Pearl Harbor had sunk battleships but no carriers. Now they must finish the work they had begun at Oahu, and Midway seemed the best place to lay a trap for American flattops.

If the Japanese command had any doubts about the plan to attack Midway, they were wiped away shortly after noon on April 18, 1942. At about noon on that day, a flight of U.S. B-25s suddenly appeared over Tokyo and bombed the Japanese capital. Damage was slight, but the psychological impact was profound both in the U.S. and Japan. Grinning broadly, President Roosevelt told the world the big land-based bombers had flown from "Shangri-la." The truth was hardly less fantastic. Actually, the Army Air Corps B-25s, under the command of Colonel James H. Doolittle, had taken off from the deck of an aircraft carrier, the USS *Hornet*.

The bombing shocked and deeply offended the Japanese public. Tokyo, where the Emperor lived in his walled Chrysanthemum Palace, was the very heart and soul of Japan. Admiral Yamamoto, who was charged with protecting the Emperor, was aghast. Yamamoto and other Japanese commanders understood only too well that they owed this insult not to mythical Shangri-la, but to the U.S. carrier fleet. Now they were determined to snare the American carriers and sink them—at Midway.

Bombs and torpedos finish the Imperial Navy carrier *Shoho* on May 7, 1942, during the Battle of the Coral Sea. Striking at one another with planes instead of shells, the warships of the two fleets never sighted one another. The U.S. lost the USS *Lexington*, and history's first all-out carrier-against-carrier battle ended in a draw.

The Japanese battle plan for Midway had one serious flaw—a fatal one, as it turned out. As with any trap, success could only be achieved if the quarry was deceived and fell into the net. What the Japanese did not know was that the U.S. Navy had turned the tables and arranged an ambush of their own. In one of the most extraordinary intelligence breakthroughs in history, the Americans had cracked the Imperial Navy's code. They knew the broad outlines of Yamamoto's plan and even some of its details. They knew the Japanese were coming, knew they planned to attack the Aleutian Islands first as a diversion and then lie in wait off Midway to pounce on the Americans—who would be hurrying, too late, to defend that strategic island.

The Japanese submarines deployed in a long line to watch for the American carriers, but they waited in vain. The U.S. fleet sailed around the line of enemy subs and took up a position to the northeast of Midway, out of range of Japanese carrier-based reconnaissance aircraft. Meanwhile scout planes based on an unsinkable carrier—Midway with its airstrip—scoured the ocean searching for Yamamoto's enormous fleet.

Admiral Yamamoto's Midway armada consisted of three main battle groups. Under Admiral Nagumo, the advance group included the carriers *Akagi, Kaga, Soryu,* and *Hiryu*; all had taken part in the attack on Pearl Harbor half a year earlier. Also under Nagumo's command were two battleships, six heavy cruisers, and an occupation force of 5,000 men in twelve transports, as well as sixteen submarines and a scattering of destroyers to provide a screen. Admiral

Chapter Two • MIDWAY

Yamamoto followed Nagumo with a second powerful force including three of Japan's newest battleships, four older battleships, and a light cruiser. Plowing through heavy fog to the northeast was the third battle group. This was the diversionary force consisting of two light carriers, two heavy cruisers, and four large transports loaded with troops to occupy the Aleutian Islands of Adak, Attu, and Kiska.

Including tenders and small patrol vessels, the Japanese fleet numbered 162 vessels. Admiral Chester W. Nimitz had at his disposal a force of only seventy-six warships, and about a third of these were in the northern Pacific, far from the main theater of battle near Midway. The airstrip at Midway gave American forces some additional punch with 115 fighters, bombers, and torpedo planes.

Both sides were girded for battle, and at dawn on June 4 the contest began. At about 6:00 A.M. a Navy float plane flying out of Midway reported two

One month after the Coral Sea battle, the opposing carrier fleets met again, this time at Midway. Having broken the Imperial Navy code, U.S. commanders were aware of Japanese plans to attack the atoll and sent three carriers to ambush the enemy task force. A U.S. dive bomber prepares for take-off.

Among those who died at Midway was Lieutenant Commander John Waldron, torpedo bomber squadron leader from the *Hornet*. The U.S. torpedo planes were the first to go in against the enemy carriers, but their suicidal attack proved unsuccessful. All but a few were cut to pieces by fighters and antiaircraft fire, and only a handful of the young pilots and crewmen survived.

Japanese carriers approaching the island from the southeast. Rear Admiral Frank Jack Fletcher on the USS *Yorktown,* which was recovering planes from a search mission, ordered the *Hornet* and *Enterprise,* under Rear Admiral Raymond A. Spruance, to head southwesterly at battle speed and attack. *Yorktown* would catch up.

Meanwhile, radar on Midway picked up a mass of aircraft racing straight for the island. These were 108 Japanese planes from Admiral Nagumo's carriers sent to knock out the Midway airstrip. As a counterpunch, four waves of American planes took off from Midway to bomb the enemy fleet, but they did little damage. The Japanese bombers hit Midway at 6:30 A.M., drubbing it for a full 20 minutes, but when they flew off again, the island's runways remained intact. Having failed to destroy the airstrip, the attack could not be considered a success. As yet unaware of the presence nearby of U.S. carriers, Nagumo ordered another strike on Midway. This would prove a fatal error.

Officers in Spruance's fleet guessed that Nagumo would now decide to launch a second Midway strike. Calculating the time the Japanese would need to recover, refuel, and rearm their planes, Spruance launched an immediate all-out

While the torpedo planes kept the Japanese busy below, the U.S. Navy dive bombers moved into position overhead. Among the most historic combat photographs ever taken, this picture shows U.S. warplanes about to drop down on enemy carriers off Midway. Smoke trails from a burning ship, probably a carrier. The Japanese lost four large carriers in the battle, all to dive-bomb attack. The calamitous defeat forced the Imperial Navy onto the defensive for the rest of the war.

attack intended to catch Nagumo's carriers at a particularly vulnerable moment—with bombs and fuel lines strewn across their decks. Spruance let go twenty Wildcat fighters, sixty-seven Dauntless dive bombers, and twenty-seven Devastator torpedo bombers.

The Japanese ships had changed course since being sighted earlier, and the war birds had a hard time finding them. Running perilously low on fuel, they were about to turn back when a cloud bank beneath them parted to reveal Nagumo's huge carrier fleet. When the pilots radioed back to their own carriers that they had found the enemy, Spruance left no doubt about what was to happen next. "Attack!" he said. "Attack immediately."

Although hit hard by American bombers, the Japanese fleet launched a furious counterattack. Struck by a 5-inch antiaircraft shell, an attacking Japanese Jill disintegrates. Notice the torpedo falling from the plane.

Another Jill explodes and crashes.

Chapter Two • MIDWAY

The final desperate Japanese blows at Midway fell on the *Yorktown*. Struck by a pair of torpedos, the big carrier lists dramatically to starboard. Two days after the battle, an enemy submarine sank her.

The torpedo squadrons, which were well out ahead of the dive bombers, were the first to go in. Diving down to wave level in wedge–shaped formations, one squadron after another charged the Japanese carriers. But they had been assigned an impossible task. The lumbering torpedo planes were easy targets for antiaircraft guns on the Japanese ships, and they were jumped from left, right, and above by fire-spitting Zero fighters. It has been said that no Japanese kamikaze pilot ever went into battle with more certainty of being killed than the young Americans who crewed the torpedo planes at Midway. All but a few of the planes were knocked down long before they got close enough to launch their torpedos. Only four made it back to their carriers, and among the crews of the downed torpedo planes only a single pilot survived. But those who were killed had not died in vain.

The torpedo attacks had kept the Japanese antiaircraft gunners and fighter planes busy while the American dive bombers moved unnoticed into position overhead. Little more than a minute after the last hapless torpedo plane struck

Devoid of air cover, the Japanese fleet took terrible punishment at Midway. U.S. bombers made a smoldering wreck of this heavy cruiser.

the water, the dive bombers screamed down on the *Soryu, Kaga,* and *Akagi.* Just as Spruance had hoped, they had caught the Japanese carriers in a fatally vulnerable condition, with refueling and rearming airplanes all over their decks. In moments all three carriers were turned into enormous torches.

It was not yet 10:30 in the morning, and already Japanese hopes for victory at Midway had gone up in smoke. Nonetheless Nagumo kept fighting, and ordered planes from his remaining carrier, the *Hiryu,* into the air. By following American planes as they returned to their carriers, Japanese attack squadrons located the *Yorktown.* Known affectionately to her crew as "Waltzing Matilda," the *Yorktown* had been seriously damaged several weeks earlier at the Battle of the Coral Sea. Japanese pilots were sure they had sunk her. Now they swooped down to finish the job. Two torpedos slashed through the water and struck the *Yorktown,* and the explosions seemed to lift the big carrier completely out of the water. Before dark U.S. bombers would avenge the attack on the *Yorktown* by blasting the *Hiryu* and forcing the thoroughly discouraged Nagumo into retreat.

While the roaring brawl was taking place on the surface and in the air under a porcelain blue Pacific sky, the *Nautilus* prowled the ocean depths searching for opportunities to hurt the enemy. McKinley was at his starboard station in the forward torpedo room when the submarine made contact with a Japanese battle-

Chapter Two • MIDWAY

Admiral Chester W. Nimitz, architect of the American victory at Midway.

ship. The *Nautilus* loosed torpedos at the huge ship, which began zig-zagging to avoid them. Then, while the torpedos were still racing toward their target, the *Nautilus* was also forced to take evasive action. Japanese destroyers were rushing toward the *Nautilus*; the hunter had become the hunted.

American carrier crewmen taking a well deserved, if precarious, nap under a bright Pacific sun.

Exploding depth charges pounded and shook the *Nautilus* as the submarine dove deeper and deeper. This was McKinley's first time under depth-charge attack, and he was terrified. The shock of the explosions shook the deck under the crew's feet as *Nautilus* continued down. Dust fell from cable runs, overheads, and light bulbs, which would flicker off and on, and pieces of cork insulation popped off the interior of the hull and fell. Worst of all, leaks opened up and the crew scrambled to close them. In spite of the horrible din, crewmen worked in silence for fear that any sound might help the enemy pinpoint their position. Finally the nearly constant drumbeat of explosions came to an end.

The *Nautilus* waited, listened, and then returned to periscope depth. There were several ships on the horizon, but one in particular caught the captain's eye. She was a Japanese aircraft carrier, apparently damaged but still underway. "We fired three torpedos and started the stop watch," said McKinley. "Then we heard a click [a detonator] followed by two explosions."

Although the *Nautilus* came under depth-charge attack by the carrier's destroyer escorts, the submarine remained close to its huge target. "We stuck around all day," said McKinley. "Then the escort left, and we came back up again. The carrier was burning and listing down by the bow. Since no escort was around, we could afford a pretty good look. The captain called the torpedomen to the conning tower, one at a time, to see what we had done. It was one of the most vivid sights I have ever seen. Jap carriers had open bows with V-shaped supports forward, so I had no trouble identifying it as I had the planes at Pearl Harbor.

"That night we heard a whole series of explosions, and then creaking and groaning noises. The sounds were made by the breaking and flooding of a sinking ship. I believe it was the *Soryu*.

"We put back into Midway. The battle was over."

The era of Japanese military expansion was also over. Midway had been a disaster of almost unimaginable proportions for Japan. Having lost four carriers, over 250 planes, most of their best pilots, and more than 2,400 officers and men, the Imperial Navy would be forced to fight on the defensive for the rest of the war. Captain Mitsuo Fuchida, who led the Pearl Harbor air strike, was wounded while abandoning the blazing *Akagi*. Once back in Japan he and other Midway wounded were hospitalized in seclusion and the Japanese public was not told about the defeat at Midway.

But for McKinley and every other American, the battle was cause for elation. Only six months before, McKinley had stood on a finger pier in Pearl Harbor, firing a World War I rifle at Japanese torpedo planes. Now he had helped sink one of the carriers that launched the air strike on Pearl Harbor. "Some say we didn't hit the carrier. But I remember the explosions after we fired the torpedos, and I remember looking through the periscope at a carrier on fire and going down...."

Chapter Three

GUADALCANAL: Terror in the Night

White sand, warm sun, coconut palm fronds swaying in an ocean breeze—the isles of the South Pacific have long been compared with paradise. But to thousands of Americans who fought in the Pacific during World War II, these idyllic atolls and volcanic islands suggest nothing so much as hell. One such veteran is Bill Davis. His descent into hell began on a particularly dark night in the fall of 1942, and started with a blinding flash of light.

Stationary Carriers

Following the defeat at Pearl Harbor, the battered U.S. Navy lacked the strength necessary for a direct and decisive strike at Japan. American military planners recognized that winning the war in the east would be a gradual process. Victory could only be achieved one step at a time, and in the Pacific, by far the largest body of water on earth, most of those steps would be taken on islands. The American strategy in the Pacific has often been described as "island hopping." The idea was to establish a foothold in an island chain, clear it of the enemy, and then use it as a secure base for an advance into the next chain. Airstrips, hurriedly cleared by Seabee construction teams, would convert cap-

Deep in the Guadalcanal jungles, a Marine cleans his rifle beside a makeshift dwelling.

tured islands almost overnight into stationary aircraft carriers. And each archipelago seized by U.S. forces would move American bombers a few hundred miles closer to Japan.

It was a sensible strategy, one that took advantage of America's ability to build more ships and produce more war materiel than its enemy. But of course, the plan had to work not just on paper or on a map, but out in the ocean and on tiny atolls hardly bigger than a city park. And it was U.S. sailors, airmen, Marines, and soldiers who would have to make it work. The first major test of the strategy came at Guadalcanal in the fall of 1942, and ironically, it was the Japanese who struck the first blow.

The Imperial Navy was pursuing an island strategy of its own. By establishing bases and airfields in New Guinea and the Solomon Islands, Japan could place its ships and bombers within easy striking distance of Australia. After the fall of the Philippines, U.S. and Allied forces had fallen back on Australia to regroup, and several key supply bases were located in the north of that country. Success in the Solomons might enable the Japanese to sever the U.S. Navy's vital Australian supply lines. Perhaps the boldest and most threatening Japanese move in the Solomons was their attempt, beginning in the summer of 1942, to build an airstrip on Guadalcanal.

Learning the Japanese were building an air base on Guadalcanal, the U.S. rushed an invasion force to that strategic South Pacific island. Marines fought their way ashore on many enemy-held islands in the Solomons.

Chapter Three • GUADALCANAL   41

News of an enemy air base under construction on this key island brought an almost immediate response by the American command. The potential threat of Japanese bombers on Guadalcanal was too great to ignore, and a major amphibious assault force was rushed to the Solomons. At first light on August 7, an armada of U.S. warships began to pound enemy positions on the island. Three hours later, Marines were streaming onto the beaches and pushing into the Guadalcanal jungle. Soon they had overrun their primary objective—the unfinished Japanese airfield. Construction crews set to work on the landing strip, and within days, U.S. warplanes were roaring down the runway to hit the enemy from the air. The new air base was renamed Henderson Field, and it would play a crucial role in the bloody eight-month tug-of-war over Guadalcanal.

This fierce back-and-forth struggle featured several of the sharpest naval surface engagements of the entire war. Most of the ship-to-ship fighting took place at night between a series of adjacent islands in a relatively narrow passage known to the American side as "the Slot." Later both sides would begin to call

Death agonies of the *Wasp*. On September 15, 1942, while supporting operations on Guadalcanal, the carrier was fatally wounded by a Japanese submarine. Three "Long Lance" torpedos struck the *Wasp*. Three others missed the flattop and raced on nearly a dozen miles through the ocean before sinking a U.S. destroyer and seriously damaging the battleship *North Carolina*.

the passage "Iron Bottom Sound" because of the extraordinary number of warships sunk there.

Menaced by land-based planes from Henderson Field, Japanese battle flotillas avoided daylight engagements, but they were fearless at night. The Imperial Navy had trained its crews in night-fighting techniques, and no navy has ever performed better in the dark. The Japanese swept down the Slot repeat-

A "Long Lance" torpedo knocked this gaping hole in the 35,000-ton USS *North Carolina*.

edly, always under cover of darkness. The Americans had the advantage of radar, but in spite of this, they were all too often caught by surprise and unprepared for an attack. When fighting in the Slot reached a climax on the night of November 13, 1942, the U.S. fleet was once again caught off guard.

David and Goliath

That night the shock of combat hit Bill Davis with brutal suddenness. It came in a painful flash of hot, white light that stung his eyes and sent a shot of adrenaline racing through his veins. The searchlight of a Japanese battlewagon had found Davis' tin can, the destroyer *Laffey*. Like a monster out of a medieval Japanese myth, the battleship *Hei* had unexpectedly materialized out of the dark Pacific mists. Now it was closing in on the *Laffey*, threatening to slice her in half.

The destroyer *Laffey* loaded with survivors from the torpedoed *Wasp*. Two months later the *Laffey* itself became the victim of a Japanese torpedo.

From his battle station, a 20mm gun mount on the starboard side, Davis could see the huge Japanese ship bearing down on him and his small ship. For a few gut-wrenching seconds, Davis was sure the two ships would collide—with predictably calamitous results. They didn't. But the destroyer's troubles were just beginning. The *Laffey* was now locked in a duel to the finish with an enemy ship twenty times her size and with more than twenty times her firepower. The *Laffey* displaced about 2,200 tons; the *Hei* displaced more than *45,000* tons. The *Laffey*'s hardest-hitting guns were 5-inchers; the *Hei*'s biggest guns were the size of tree trunks and could fire 14-inch shells. As the giant battleship surged by just 75 feet away, Davis found himself staring straight down the barrel of one of those 14-inch guns. "I am going to die right now," he thought.

Fortunately for the American ship and her embattled crew, the *Hei* was much too close to bring its big guns to bear on the destroyer. But the Japanese blazed away with their antiaircraft and machine guns—and Davis and his fellow gunners blazed back. Bullets hammered at Davis's gun shield, and his friend Bob Sims in an adjacent gun mount was hit and killed. But Davis kept firing.

A marine tank heads for Guadalcanal.

Having seized the Japanese airstrip on Guadalcanal, U.S. forces used it to take command of the skies over the Solomons. A B-17 "Flying Fortress" on an island bombing mission

The Japanese tried repeatedly to reinforce their besieged garrison on Guadalcanal. Grim evidence of one such effort, a Japanese troop ship lies sunk by the stern.

Gnawing at the enemy ship with his 20mm, he first darkened the hateful searchlight, then turned his attention to the bridge, the nerve center of the enemy ship. "My shells were chewing up the flash shield around the bridge as if it were canvas," said Davis, who was so close to his target that "the sound of the shot and the sound of the shell hitting the bridge were inseparable."

Miraculously, it seemed the American David was winning its battle with the Japanese Goliath—but only for a moment. As the *Hei* moved away into the darkness, the barrels of her enormous guns leveled with the destroyer. What happened next has never been entirely clear. The U.S. ship began to take heavy fire from both port and starboard. Then there was a tremendous explosion. Some say a 14-inch shell from the *Hei* had found its mark. Others, including Davis, believe the *Laffey* was hit by a "Long Lance" torpedo fired from a nearby Japanese destroyer. Whatever its source, the wound proved fatal.

Davis woke up in a life raft more than 50 feet from his gun mount. His shoes were gone and his mouth was filled with the strong taste of brass. All around him were dead sailors, and he heard the cries of others who were dying. "Sick bay....Sick bay....Martha....Mother."

The *Laffey* itself was dying. The explosion had started a hundred fires, and there was no longer the manpower or the water pressure needed to put them out. The ship's skipper, Lieutenant Commander William Hank, saw the situation was

American air strength in the Solomons forced the Imperial Navy to do most of its fighting at night, something the Japanese had trained for extensively. They pounded the U.S. fleet in a series of sharp night actions off Guadalcanal. Shells and tracer bullets cut deadly streaks through the darkness.

Chapter Three • GUADALCANAL

The five Sullivan brothers went down together when the cruiser *Juneau* was lost on November 13, 1942, during the naval Battle of Guadalcanal

hopeless and reluctantly ordered his men over the side. The skipper lowered the ship's dog, a mongrel named Chafing Gear (C.G. for short) into a whaleboat. With C.G. safely in the boat, Hank turned to Davis, who happened to be standing nearby. "Well," Hank shouted at the stunned seaman, "go!"

"Aren't you coming, Captain?" asked Davis.

"Of course, I'm coming," snapped Hank. Then the skipper hurried off toward the bow and disappeared into the smoke. Davis never saw him again.

Grabbing a line dangling from a whaleboat davit, Davis swung out and dropped into the ocean. He found the water foul-tasting and covered with oil. The destroyer's fuel tanks had ruptured, the fire was burning higher and higher, and it was obvious the ship's magazines and depth charges would blow up at any moment. There was nothing to do but swim away as fast as he could. "I took off at flank speed," said Davis.

When the explosion came, it obliterated the entire stern of the ship. Hot metal and burning bits of mattresses rained onto the men in the water, who watched the destroyer point her bow skyward and then slip down into Iron Bottom Sound. Davis and several dozen other splashing, gasping survivors braved the waves until about 10:00 o'clock the next day when a boat from Guadalcanal rescued them.

Many other sailors, both American and Japanese, were not so lucky that night. The toll of ships and men lost during this battle in the dark was among the highest in the war. Davis would later learn, to his horror, that fifty-six of his shipmates had gone to the bottom with the *Laffey*. Another 110 American sailors were lost when enemy guns pummeled and sank the destroyer *Monssen*. So many Japanese shells—the Navy report said thirty-seven—struck the *Monssen* that its crew lost count. Also badly hit was the destroyer *Cushing,* which sank with a loss of seventy-one officers and men. Nearly the entire crew of the *Barton* was lost when a brace of enemy torpedos sliced through the night and cut the destroyer in half. Early on the morning after the battle, the cruiser *Juneau* was lined up in the crosshairs of a Japanese submarine periscope. The enemy sub pumped at least two torpedos into the *Juneau*, shattering her hull and sending her

Having secured Guadalcanal, U.S. forces pushed on through the South Pacific wresting one sandy atoll after another from the stubborn Japanese. One of the hardest fights came at Tarawa during November, 1943. A Marine takes on a Japanese pillbox.

Chapter Three • GUADALCANAL

to the bottom with all but a few of her crew members. Among those who went down with the cruiser were five young sailors from the same family, the Sullivan brothers.

There were also severe losses on the Japanese side and several ships from the Imperial fleet were added to the wreckage rusting on the bottom of Iron Bottom Sound. The heaviest loss was the mammoth battleship *Hei*. As it turned out, the giant ship had been seriously wounded during its shoot-out with the overmatched *Laffey*. Fire from the destroyer, perhaps from Bill Davis's gun mount, had heavily damaged the *Hei*'s bridge and killed many of her officers. Even Vice Admiral Hiroaki Abe was wounded during the exchange. Slowed by the damage, the *Hei* was caught out in the open when the sun came up the next morning. That made her easy prey for Henderson Field bomber squadrons, which pounded her in one angry wave after another. Shortly before noon she went down—just as the *Laffey* had—stern first.

A beach on Tarawa.

Crossing the T

It took almost eight months for U.S. forces to wrest Guadalcanal from the stubborn Japanese. Meanwhile, the island-hopping campaign moved up the Solomon chain, with the enemy fighting fiercely for each jungle, mountain, and spit of sand. The two navies clashed again and again in the seas between the islands.

"Sometimes it would be a real shoot-out," said Peter Black, who served in the Solomons aboard the light cruiser *St. Louis*.

Black had graduated from Harvard on June 5, 1942, while fighting raged near Midway and in the Aleutians. Within weeks he was on his way to the Aleutians himself. Ensign Black was to serve as assistant navigator on the *St. Louis*, at that time assigned to the Northern Pacific Fleet on patrol in the Bering Sea. "You've never seen such weather," said Black. "We had storms, fog, rain, and cold, even in the summer."

No man is an island.

Sailors aboard the *St. Louis* had not been issued cold-weather gear, so "When we were in port, we all went out and bought overcoats," Black said.

Eventually, the crew of the *St. Louis* received an enormous shipment of arctic parkas and other cold-weather clothing—but by that time the cruiser had been sent to the Solomon Islands in the tropics. Here in the South Pacific the weather was not the only thing that was hot. So was the action.

At the battle of Kula Gulf, a torpedo fired by a Japanese destroyer almost blew off the bow of the *St. Louis*. "I was standing on the bridge when we were hit," said Black. "My first thought was that I didn't have on a life jacket. The young officers considered it sporty to go around without them. Now I was sorry I didn't have mine, because I certainly didn't want to go swimming around the Solomons without one."

The *St. Louis* had been badly hit, but she did not sink. Repair crews welded a makeshift wedge of metal onto the front of the cruiser, and she limped back to the U.S. for a new bow. Then she returned to the fray.

Black fought for three years in the Pacific, and he saw plenty of action. He saw a Japanese cruiser go down after it lost a duel with the *St. Louis*. He saw the *Helena*—sister ship of the *St. Louis*—explode and sink after she was torpedoed. At Bougainville he saw clusters of enemy shells hit the water all around the *St. Louis*, throwing up water spouts like a school of whales. Near Rabaul he locked eyes with the pilot of a Japanese bomber as it screamed just over the cruiser's deck and crashed into the sea. "I thought he was coming straight for my head," Black said. "He hit us with a bomb and started a fire. We had to go down into the magazine and carry up 40mm rounds that were so hot they burned our hands. We threw them over the side."

But it was the fight at Kula Gulf, where his ship took a torpedo hit, that Black remembered best. "We crossed the T of the Japanese column," he recalled. "It's an old naval tactic. Admiral Nelson used it at Trafalgar. Even the Greeks did it back when they were throwing rocks at one another."

Black finished the war as a Lieutenant Commander and navigator aboard the *Marcus Island*, an escort carrier. Perhaps because of his experience at Kula Gulf, he has been a lifelong fan of Admiral Nelson and his tactics. Many years after he left the Navy, Black sailed to the Mediterranean on his yacht, the *Caroline*. There he visited the site of the Battle of Trafalgar where Nelson "crossed the T" of an enormous French fleet and ended Napoleon's attempt to dominate the seas.

Chapter Four

NORTH ATLANTIC: The U-boat War

A victim of the U-boat wolf packs.

The fight for the Atlantic was a war of nerves and of terrors. Stalking the heavily traveled sea-lanes in deadly wolf packs, German U-boats exacted an awful toll on Allied shipping. Sailors never knew when or where the wolves would move in for the kill. The Allies fought back with sonar-equipped destroyers, sub-killing patrol aircraft, and depth charges so powerful that even one could crush the hull of a submarine.

It was a fight of unparalleled viciousness in which death approached unseen out of the dark and struck like lightning. Both sides suffered enormous losses. In all, the U-boats would sink 2,575 Allied and neutral merchant vessels carrying a total of 14.5 million tons of cargo. Down with them went more than 30,000 British and 15,000 American merchant seamen in addition to thousands of naval officers and men. In turn, the Allies sent to the bottom 781 U-boats along with more than 30,000 German officers and men. About three-quarters of the German sailors who served on U-boats were killed in action or captured.

The sea war that became known as the Battle of the Atlantic raged from the ice-strewn Arctic to the edge of the Southern Ocean, pressed in close to the East Coast of North America, spilled into the Caribbean, and even found its way into the warm waters of the Gulf of Mexico. It was a war people could watch from the shore, as the German subs torpedoed coast-hugging merchant ships within sight of public beaches and seaside resorts. And it was a war fought in mid-ocean where wolf packs closed in on huge merchant convoys bound for Great Britain or Russia.

Once America had officially entered the war, German U-boats pounced on shipping along the eastern seaboard. This merchant vessel was torpedoed within sight of the U.S. coast.

Powerful radio transmitters on shore made it possible for commanders to keep in constant contact with the combatants, and this had the effect of turning millions of square miles of ocean into one gigantic chessboard. Germany's Admiral Karl Doenitz, a former World War I U-boat commander, plotted strategy from his headquarters in occupied Paris. Working around the clock in plotting rooms of their own in Washington, London, and Liverpool, the Allies tried to contain Doenitz's U-boats and limit the damage they did to convoys. But once the strategy on either side had been shaped, it was the men at sea who had to carry it out.

The U-boats, many of which operated out of occupied French ports, were sometimes guided to their targets by intelligence information revealing the course and the number of ships in a convoy. The first U-boat to make contact would trail astern of the convoy, radioing its position. Paris would then relay the position to other U-boats at sea, a wolf pack would gather, and the carnage would begin.

Chapter Four • NORTH ATLANTIC

The Allies tried to minimize the damage to shipping through use of the escorted convoy system. Up to sixty vessels of varying sizes and seaworthiness were herded into convoys and organized into columns that reached from horizon to horizon. The pace was set by the slowest vessels. Harried escorts ran to and fro beside the convoys, keeping stragglers in formation as best they could while constantly hunting for U-boats. The hunt was aided by asdic (sonar), radar, and high frequency direction finders (HF/DF). The Germans countered with METOX, a device that detected radar frequencies.

Usually, U-boats attacked at night on the surface. Their daring commanders ran right into the middle of the convoys, maneuvering skillfully and loosing torpedos at the largest vessels they could find. These bold tactics were enormously risky. At any moment a bright flare or star shell might turn night into day, allowing the deck guns on the merchant ships to blaze away at the illuminated U-boats.

To protect freighters, the Allies organized large convoys and guarded them with destroyer escorts. Here an escort drops depth charges on a suspected enemy submarine. Notice the convoy ships on the horizon.

Less daring U-boat commanders lurked in the darkness at the edge of the convoys and fired spreads of several torpedos hoping that one or more of them would find a target. When an escort approached, they dove.

Although heavily loaded with depth charges and detection equipment, the escorts frequently did double duty as rescue ships. In the icy North Atlantic, a man could live in the water for only a few minutes before dying from the cold.

Some depth charges contained hundreds of pounds of explosive, and the shock waves they created could tear a submerged U-boat apart.

When a ship was torpedoed and sunk, the escorts hurried to the scene to fish desperate survivors out of the freezing water or pull them aboard from tossing lifeboats.

Bloody Winter

Winter in the North Atlantic is synonymous with horrible weather. The days are short and the skies crowded with gun-gray clouds. Even worse than most was the so-called Bloody Winter of 1942–43, when fierce Arctic storms and blood-freezing temperatures competed with the wolf packs to destroy ships and men. As the Bloody Winter set in, the U-boats were winning their fight to choke off the flow of oil, supplies, and foodstuffs to Great Britain. By mid-winter British leaders estimated the island had food enough for only about three more months.

The lightly protected, slow-moving convoys on the North Atlantic runs made juicy targets for the U-boats. Ships were going down faster than they could be replaced. The thinly stretched British provided all the convoy escorts they could, but many more were needed. The U.S. Navy, caught with fewer ships than it needed to fight a two-ocean war, pressed into service its old World War I destroyers. Shortly before the declaration of war, the Coast Guard had been integrated into the Navy, and its Hamilton Class cutters were quickly placed on convoy escort duty.

"Hedgehog" depth charges such as these were fired in a pattern two dozen or more at a time. A hit by even one might fatally wound a submarine.

Killing a U-boat

Little more than a week before Christmas in 1942, assistant gunnery officer John Waters was standing a night watch aboard the Coast Guard Cutter *Ingham*. Only the day before, the *Ingham* and two other fighting ships had joined a fifty-vessel, eastbound convoy labeled SC-112. A wolf pack had been forming around the convoy and was taking exploratory bites. To help fight off the U-boats, the three ships had been rushed from Iceland to reinforce the escorts already struggling to protect the convoy. *Ingham* took up a position beside the column of merchant ships and, using sonar, radar, and high frequency radio direction finders, began searching for the enemy. On the evening of December 17, a contact was made. Somewhere nearby was a German submarine.

Waters had had little combat experience. He had just graduated from the United States Coast Guard Academy at New London, Connecticut. Born and raised on the coast of North Carolina, he had attended North Carolina State on a football scholarship. Waters thought briefly about professional football, but could not see much future in it. Besides, he liked water better than turf. He knew a war was coming and wanted to be in it, so in spite of his love for the ocean, he joined the Army National Guard. Meanwhile, he also applied for a Congressional appointment to the U.S. Military Academy at West Point and took a competitive examination for admission to the Coast Guard Academy.

Often convoy escorts were called upon to rescue survivors from torpedoed merchant vessels. These U.S. Navy destroyer crewmen are preparing a net to help foundering seamen board their ship.

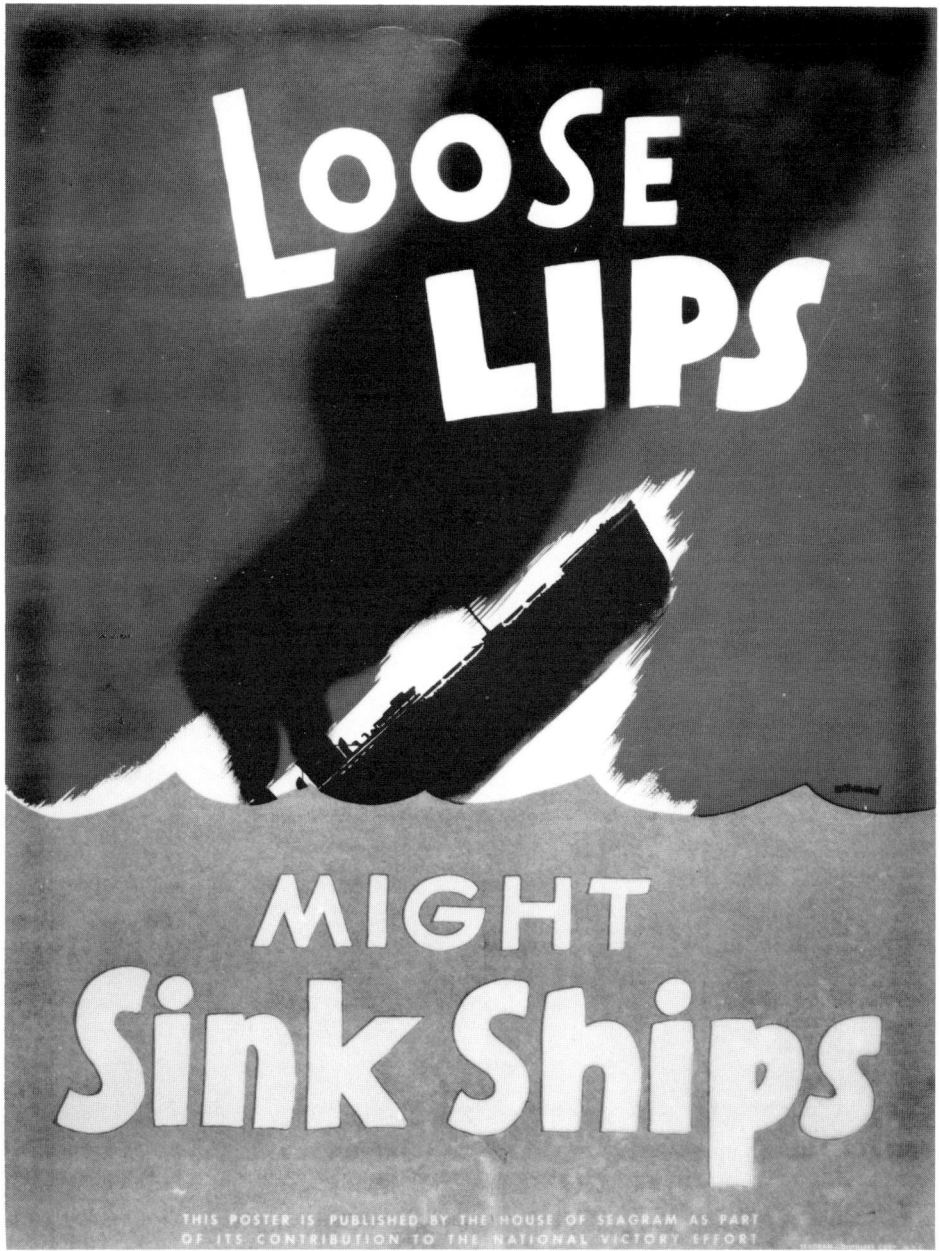

To make it harder for the enemy to gather intelligence on shipments and convoys, officials clamped a tight security lid over docks and shipyards.

In 1939, Waters received simultaneous appointments to both schools. He had not anticipated such a choice, and it was not an easy one to make. He had just returned from three weeks of muddy maneuvers in Mississippi with the Third Army, and he asked his National Guard colonel which academy he should choose. To the colonel, whose military career had been in the Army, the choice was a simple one. Did Waters want to eat his meals out of a mess kit in the field or would he prefer dining at a table fitted with a white tablecloth? That did it. Waters had just spent three weeks picking leaves and twigs from his rain-spat-

Constant air patrols helped locate U-boats so that bombers and destroyers could sink them.

tered mess kit. He chose the Coast Guard Academy. Waters was in the Class of 1943, but that class was graduated a year early because of the war. So by December of 1942 he was already serving in the Atlantic.

On only his third night at sea, Waters was roughly initiated into the hard business of war. He and another ensign were sharing a stateroom on a cutter churning its way toward a convoy south of Iceland. The stateroom was located over the vessel's starboard screw. Waters and the other ensign were asleep when the cutter's bridge made sonar contact with what was thought to be an enemy submarine. The cutter dropped a 600-pound depth charge off the stern. When it exploded, only about a hundred yards behind the cutter, the impact lifted the sleeping ensigns completely out of their bunks and threw them onto the deck. Waters hit the deck first, and the ensign in the bunk above—another former football player and heavier than Waters—crashed down on top of him. For a moment they were convinced they had been torpedoed. When they found out otherwise, the young ensigns understood why their stateroom had not been taken by senior officers.

Weeks later, on the night of December 17, Waters was once more about to feel the shock of exploding depth charges, but this time he was ready. The *Ingham* shook, rattled, and rolled as its port and starboard K-guns fired 300-pound depth charges and 600-pound charges were loosed from the stern. Although Waters did not know it at the time, the target of all that pounding was the *U-626*, a recently completed U-boat on its maiden combat voyage. The skipper of the *U-626* was a reserve officer named Hans Botho Bade. Before the war, Bade had been a master mariner in the German Merchant Marine. Now he was commander of a dying U-boat. The unlucky submarine had been ahead of the Allied convoy when it broke radio silence to send a contact report to U-Boat Command in France.

The signal was picked up by convoy escorts, and the *Ingham* launched an attack. The cutter made several depth-charge runs over the submarine's position, and it was probably the second run that started *U-626* on its way to the bottom. German U-Boat Command had no contact with her after that night.

Closing the Deadly Gap

Escorts and airborne sub-killers sank U-boats by the score, but German torpedos went right on slamming into Allied merchant ships. By January 1943, it was clear to the Allies that they would lose the war unless they could reduce convoy losses. The thin line of escorts had been performing heroically, but there simply were not enough of them. Air cover over the entire convoy route was essential.

The U-boats had been making it a practice to strike at the convoys in an expanse of ocean below Greenland where there was no air cover. This area was known as the Greenland Air Gap, and for merchant ships it was a particularly

Attacked from the air and disabled, a U-boat rolls helplessly in the waves.

Hit by Navy sub-killer aircraft, this U-boat is sinking. Its crew prepares to abandon ship.

deadly stretch of ocean. When the *Ingham* and other escorts entered this treacherous zone, their crews knew they would earn their pay. By the end of the Bloody Winter of 1943, the Allies were beginning to close the deadly Gap. Long-range bombers and sub-killers from new escort carriers made the Gap much safer for shipping.

By May of 1943, the course of the entire war had shifted in favor of the Allies, especially in the Atlantic, but still the U-boat war continued. Dealing with shifts in German submarine tactics required constant innovation on the part of the U.S. Navy. Some new ideas worked well while others did not. Hoping to use subs to kill subs, the Navy sent a full squadron of twelve submarines to Rosneath, Scotland—their mission to seek out and destroy U-boats. Navy career officer Lieutenant Commander Edward E. Conrad, then executive officer on the USS *Hake*, recalled it was a tough game and a fruitless one. The sub-killing effort was doomed, in Conrad's opinion, by a lack of sophisticated equipment. The *Hake* and the other boats in her squadron prowled the Atlantic for months with little success. Finally they were sent back to the United States for repairs.

Sometimes even battleships were used as convoy escorts. The fast battleship USS *Alabama* briefly pulled escort duty in the Atlantic, but like the *Hake* she never took on an enemy submarine. Turret Captain First Class John Brown served on the *Alabama* in the Atlantic and later when she was transferred to the Pacific theater. Brown remembered many U-boat alerts but he saw no action in the Atlantic. In the summer of 1943, *Alabama* was sent to Scapa Flow in the Orkney Islands to help the Royal Navy lure the mighty German battleship *Tirpitz* out of its lair in Norway. The German surface raider never took the bait.

Despite the success of Allied anti-submarine tactics, the wolf packs continued to take a fearsome toll throughout the war. A torpedo broke the back of this Allied tanker.

While Brown and Conrad saw little action in the Atlantic, Coast Guardsman Waters saw plenty. He helped fight the battle of the Bloody Winter and later escorted convoys to the Mediterranean. Slowly but surely, Waters and other young anti-submarine warriors turned the tide against the U-boats. Early in the war the U-boats had enjoyed an open season on U.S. shipping, sinking two million tons during the first six months alone. Merchant ships, silhouetted at night by lights from shoreside communities, were easy targets. (When they were asked to turn off their lights, resort communities from Atlantic City to the tip of Florida complained bitterly that the blackouts would hurt the tourist business.) But as the war continued, more and more German submarines were sent to the bottom, usually with their entire crews. The bombed-out German shipyards and war industries could not replace the losses.

For a short while during 1944 and 1945, the U-boats again haunted the U.S. coast. Their renewed forays were made possible by the snorkel, an air-intake/exhaust device which the Germans stole from the Royal Netherlands Navy. The snorkel stuck out of the water, but it was as difficult for aircraft to spot in the sea as a periscope. Fitted with an automatic closing valve to prevent

Convoys supplying Russia through the Arctic faced not only U-boat torpedos but also German bombers. An enemy plane crashed into the merchant vessel at the left causing it to explode.

sea water from entering the submarine, the snorkel allowed U-boats to use their diesel engines while submerged. Renewed sinkings of U.S. ships along the East Coast caused consternation. The scare was heightened when it was announced that the Germans had developed a robot bomb that could be launched at U.S. cities from U-boats. (The report was erroneous.) Admiral Doenitz was buying time with his snorkel-equipped U-boats, just as the Japanese had bought time with kamikazes. But time had begun to run out.

Waters, the football player, National Guardsman, and Coast Guardsman, finished the war as a destroyer escort commander, a rank he attained at the age of twenty-five. Eventually he was transferred to the Pacific where he saw duty at Okinawa and later in China. Whenever conditions permitted, he ate at a table fitted with a white tablecloth. He retired from the Coast Guard during the Vietnam War and took up yacht racing. Eventually he wrote and published a book about the Battle of the Atlantic titled *Bloody Winter*.

Chapter Five

SILENT AND DEEP: The Submarine War in the Pacific

T he afternoon sky was clear, the sea calm. The submarine USS *Hake*, operating out of Freemantle, Australia, was on the prowl in the Java Sea. Its prey was Japanese shipping, and it had found a juicy target—an unescorted oil tanker.

A fireball, tinged with smoke, leaped skyward when the *Hake*'s torpedos found their mark. All of the oiler's tanks had exploded at once. The crew had no time to lower boats, and Japanese sailors started jumping over the side with only their life jackets to keep them afloat. The *Hake* maneuvered in close to the survivors, and its crew urged them to come alongside for rescue. But the Japanese sailors clenched their fists and raised them skyward in defiance. They chose to cast their lot with the sea, rather than with their enemy. The burning hulk that had been their ship sank almost immediately and the *Hake*'s executive officer, Lieutenant Commander Edward Conrad, believed that all the crew had surely drowned. Of the many sinkings Conrad witnessed in nearly five years of submarine duty, this one stands out most vividly in his memory.

A 1938 graduate of the United States Naval Academy, Conrad attended the Navy's submarine school at New London, Connecticut. He was a professional. In the Atlantic the Allies struggled to protect convoys against submarine attack—to win the war they had to stop and defeat Hitler's U-boat offensive. But in the Pacific, the U.S. would turn the tables on its enemies and use its own submarines to cripple the Japanese merchant fleet and strangle Japan's industries.

An officer in a submerged U.S. submarine watches for the enemy through a periscope.

When the war began, Conrad was in Panama serving with a squadron of early 1920s-era S-boat submarines. With the rank of Lieutenant (j.g.), Conrad was executive officer of USS *S-11*. The electrifying news that Pearl Harbor had been bombed reached him as he was standing alongside the dock at Coco Solo on the Atlantic side of the Panama Canal. Not surprisingly, this news was followed closely by combat orders. The *S-11* and Conrad's entire squadron put to sea to take up stations in a thousand-mile arc curving into the Pacific from Panama. Their mission was to protect the Canal from the Japanese attack that many were sure would come. But the enemy never appeared.

Two years later Conrad was fighting on the other side of the Pacific as executive officer of the USS *Hake*, a new type of submarine much bigger and more powerful than the old S-boats. Operating from a base in Freemantle, the *Hake* stalked and sank Japanese shipping in the Southwest Pacific. The waters off Singapore and the Philippines were very productive hunting grounds and the *Hake* made many kills there. But to reach them from Freemantle the submarine had to transit the Dutch East Indies, the archipelago known today as Indonesia. It meant a perilous run through Lombock Strait at the eastern edge of Java, where the Japanese knew they were coming and waited. At least one U.S. submarine was sent to the bottom of Lombock Strait. (Other submariners consider the crew of a downed submarine to be "still on patrol.") The *Hake* would run the gauntlet at night on the surface, her engines at full bore.

After the disaster at Pearl Harbor, the threat of U.S. submarines helped protect Hawaii and the American west coast from an otherwise rampaging enemy. Soon, however, the U.S. sub fleet switched roles and went on the offensive. Photographed through a periscope, this Japanese destroyer has been cut in two by a torpedo.

Chapter Five • SILENT AND DEEP

The *Hake* searched continuously for enemy ships. Locating a convoy or stray merchant ship, she often waited until dark to close in for the kill. Night attacks were usually made on the surface. If there was a moon, the submarine kept out of its streaks. By 1943, U.S. submarines routinely used radar to see in the dark.

Usually, launching torpedos brought a furious counterattack. Playing hide-and-seek with enemy escorts and dodging their depth charges was a lottery with death. But it was all part of a grim game, and every submariner understood that the game had to be played. In order to sink an enemy ship, a submarine and its crew had to expose themselves to deadly vengeance.

Hiding Down Deep

Another submariner who understood how the game was played was William McKinley, who served aboard the *Nautilus* based at Pearl Harbor. The *Nautilus* baited the beast in its den, patroling the approaches to Tokyo Bay. Here no ship could be considered friendly, and the *Nautilus* operated under orders to sink any vessel within range of her torpedos. It took two weeks of running on the surface at night and submerged during the day to cross the 5,000 miles of ocean between Pearl Harbor and Japan. Then the *Nautilus* would remain off Japan until all but a few torpedos were expended. That usually took about two weeks, and then the submarine would head back to Pearl to pick up more supplies and torpedos.

Nautilus never went into Tokyo Bay. There were always plenty of targets passing through the approaches where the big submarine lurked in ambush. Each

The destroyer goes down.

A torpedoman inspects a stock of ship killers.

morning enemy ships sailed out of the bay, and *Nautilus*'s skipper went for the biggest one he could see. As soon as the torpedos were fired, a stopwatch was started to track their progress. Every member of the crew listened intently. The first sound of a hit was the distant click of the torpedo's detonator. Then came a series of explosions similar to the sound of several depth charges going off at once.

When torpedos were fired from periscope depth—about 60 feet—the *Nautilus* would immediately dive deeper to escape the determined depth-charge attacks of vengeful escorts. Early in the war, both navies had believed that 250 feet was the deepest a U.S. submarine could dive. During the Battle of Midway (June 3–6, 1942) however, the USS *Dolphin* got out of control and plunged to a depth of nearly 500 feet. Incredibly, she survived and returned to the surface. Until then, it had been thought the pressure at such a depth would crush a submarine hull like an empty can. Afterwards, American submarine skippers knew they could dive deeper. But the Japanese continued to set their depth-charge fuses for no more than 250 feet, leaving U.S. submarines plenty of depth in which to hide.

One morning off Tokyo Bay, as *Nautilus*'s skipper scanned the horizon through the periscope, he saw a destroyer charging straight for her. "Dive!" was

Chapter Five • SILENT AND DEEP

the command. As the submarine headed for the deep the destroyer slowed to listen for its quarry with sonar. The pinging sounds of a searching sonar are jumbled by the hunter's engine noise and water turbulence so a destroyer must slow down to hear the enemy. This, in turn, makes the destroyer more vulnerable to attack. Below, *Nautilus* kept her stern toward the destroyer while moving away very, very slowly, her propeller barely turning over. Her crew were in stockinged feet to keep noise to a minimum.

The destroyer kept up the hunt all afternoon, pinging on the *Nautilus* continuously, always at an angle of 180 degrees. The Japanese were dogged, but the destroyer was alone, without assistance. When the *Nautilus* skipper realized this, he headed toward the surface and from periscope depth fired two torpedos into the hapless destroyer. The *Nautilus* photographed the sinking Japanese ship, and the dramatic picture soon ran on the cover of *Life* magazine. This photograph, together with news of the Doolittle Raid on Tokyo, raised the flagging morale of the American public.

Torpedos were fired with compressed air from tubes such as these located at the stern of the USS *Becuna*. Usually a submarine's forward torpedo room had four tubes.

A Sub Almost Sinks Herself

American torpedos were fired from their tubes with compressed air. To prevent air bubbles from reaching the surface and giving away the submarine's position, torpedo tubes were fitted with a special poppet valve. This allowed compressed air to rush back into the torpedo room instead of into the sea. After firing, the torpedoman hurriedly tripped a lever to close the poppet valve and prevent the torpedo room from flooding. During one *Nautilus* combat mission, this arrangement almost led to disaster.

Nautilus was about to pounce on a large Japanese merchant vessel just then exiting Tokyo Bay. Believing that Tube No. 1 was loaded and ready, the skipper gave the command to fire, and the firing switch was turned in the conning tower.

U.S. strategists quickly recognized the value of submarines. They could sink the enemy merchant fleet and choke off Japanese military and industrial supplies. Two subs under construction at Groton, Connecticut.

Chapter Five • SILENT AND DEEP 73

A submarine is launched at a Wisconsin shipyard.

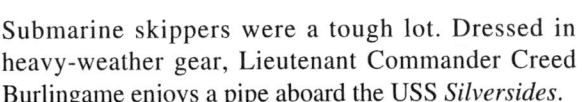

Submarine skippers were a tough lot. Dressed in heavy-weather gear, Lieutenant Commander Creed Burlingame enjoys a pipe aboard the USS *Silversides*.

Lieutenant Commander Horace Bristol and his men scan the horizon for signs of the enemy aboard the USS *Sea Dog*.

A recruitment poster takes a heroic view of submarine service.

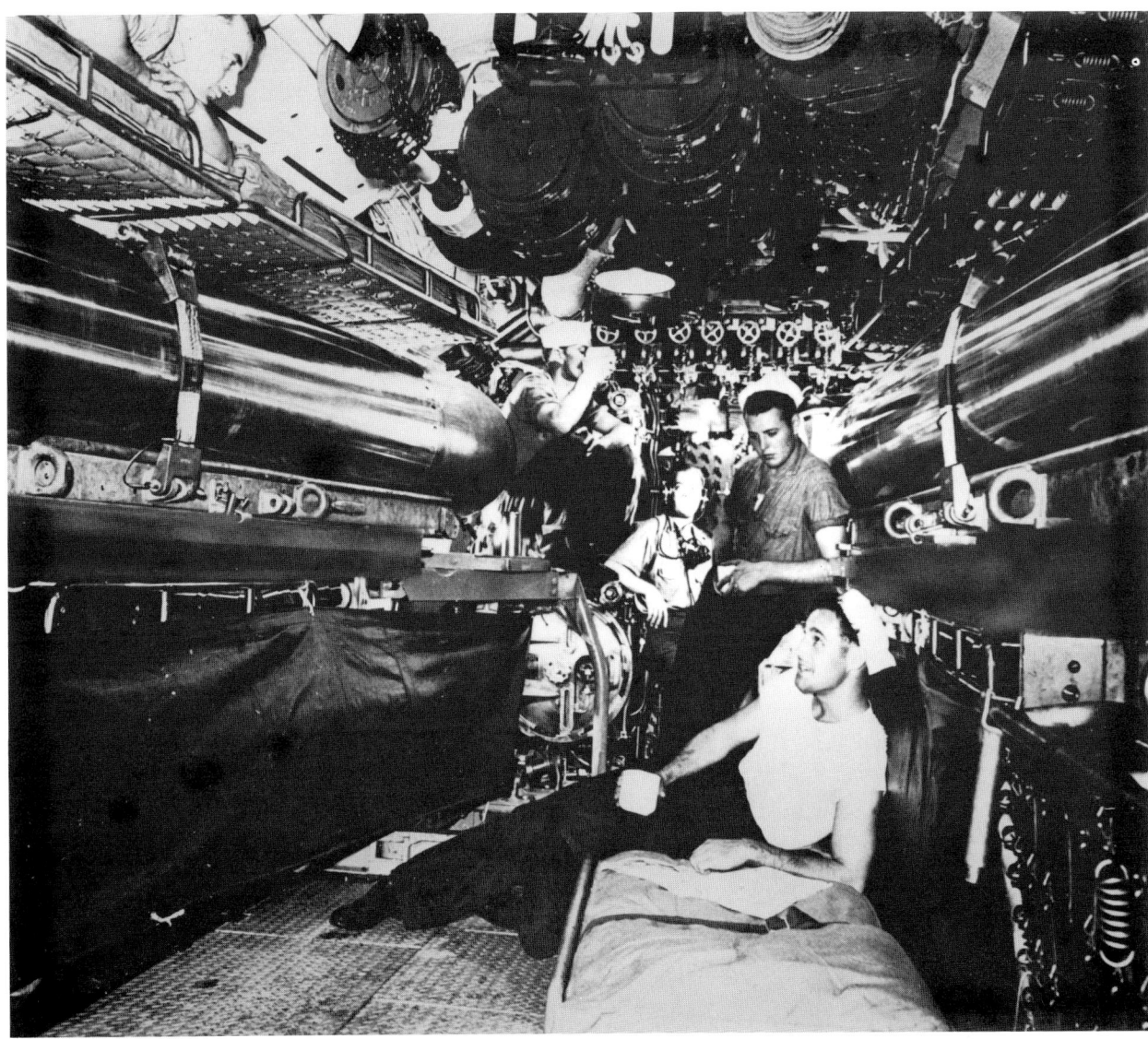

Sailors relax with coffee in a forward torpedo compartment.

Immediately, the empty tube filled with a rush of compressed air. An enemy destroyer veered toward the *Nautilus*, and the submarine went into an emergency dive. Air shooting out from the empty tube formed an enormous bubble which burst on the surface and gave away the submarine's position.

Meanwhile, a horizontal geyser of sea water gushed out of the tube into the torpedo room of the fleeing submarine. With the lights out and depth-charge explosions pounding and shaking them mercilessly, torpedoman McKinley and his mates struggled to locate and close the poppet valve. McKinley thought the *Nautilus* was badly, perhaps fatally, hit. Water was filling up the torpedo room and flooding the bilge. *Nautilus*'s bow began to turn downward. Water he could feel but not see was spraying McKinley's face as he and the other torpedomen groped for valves and levers. Finally they got the right one, and the flooding stopped just as if a spigot had been turned off.

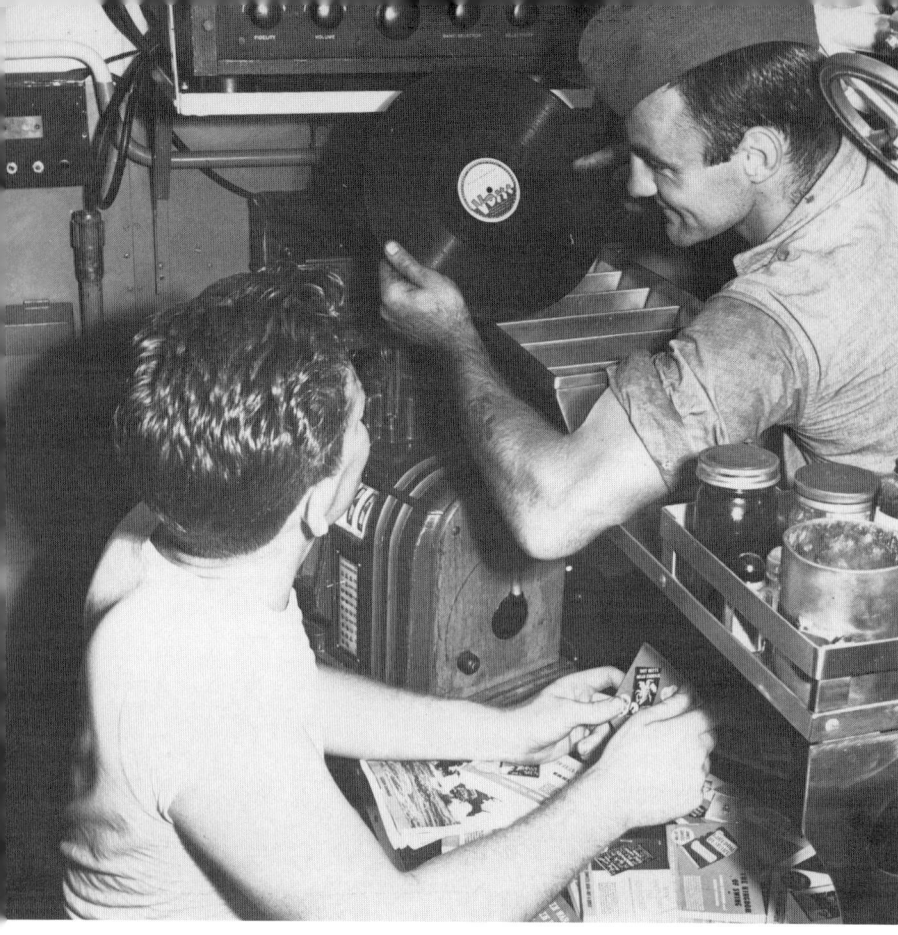

A little music, please.

A submariner enjoying a smoke, a newspaper, and the company of a friend.

Chapter Five • SILENT AND DEEP

Because their duty was so confining and dangerous, the Navy tried to give its submariners the best in comfort and relaxation when they were ashore. On one occasion, while the *Nautilus* was at Pearl Harbor, McKinley and his shipmates were whisked off to a resort hotel for poolside drinks, comfortable beds, warm breezes, and sunshine. But of course, their respite from war was only temporary.

At Pearl Harbor in early August of 1942, the *Nautilus* and a second submarine took aboard two companies of U.S. Marine Raiders and set out for Makin Island in the Gilberts. The Japanese had established a seaplane base on Makin Island as part of an intelligence-gathering operation. The Marines had been ordered to destroy the base as part of a diversion intended to draw Japanese forces away from Guadalcanal. The Marines were under the command of Lieutenant Colonel Evans F. Carlson, who had studied guerrilla tactics in China

Marines on the *Nautilus* prepare to raid an enemy base on Makin Island.

Silversides crewmen blast an enemy-held island with their deck gun.

with Mao Tse-tung. Carlson is credited with adding to the Marine Corps vocabulary a term he had borrowed from the Chinese—*Gung ho!*

At first the *Nautilus* crew was apprehensive about hauling 105 "gung ho" Marines across the Pacific. The submariner's world was an exclusive one, and before the war sailors were more used to fighting with Marines than cooperating with them. On the run to Makin, the Marines slept in shifts in jury-rigged berths aboard the crowded submarines. Sailors and Marines had to eat in shifts, too, and it seemed that people were feeding all day. While running submerged during the day, nearly everyone developed prickly heat. On the surface at night, hatches were opened to let in fresh air and to allow the Marines topside for exercise. The sailors taught the Marines how to use the submarine's head, which was operated with a complicated series of gauges, valves, and levers, and flushed outboard with a *swoosh* of compressed air. The sailors found that the Marines were fast learners, and they got along well with them. After all, they were fighting the same enemy.

Before dawn on August 17, 1942—McKinley's birthday—the *Nautilus* surfaced off Makin Island, a sandy Pacific atoll. Using inflated rubber boats, the

Chapter Five • SILENT AND DEEP

Marines hit the beach and went on the attack. Meanwhile, *Nautilus* submerged to watch the action from periscope depth. Initially, the Marine attack was a success. Then Japanese troops started pouring in on bicycles and in trucks, pinning down the two Marine companies.

Responding to a call for help, the *Nautilus* surfaced and the crew readied its forward 6-inch deck gun. Marine spotters told the *Nautilus* gunners to aim for the tallest tree on the island. But to McKinley and his fellow gunners on the deck of the submarine, all the trees looked about the same height. So the captain chose an arbitrary point on the island and told the gunnery officer to lob a shell at it. The deck gun boomed, and its 65-pound shell hit the island, sending sand, dirt, and pieces of palm tree skyward. A Marine reported the result by radio: a clear miss. But using the first shot as a point of reference, the *Nautilus* gunners began to "walk" their shells over to the enemy.

Several times the *Nautilus* had to dive to avoid attack by Japanese warplanes sent from a nearby island. Apparently the enemy had not anticipated having a submarine as their target and they carried no depth charges. When the planes were gone, the *Nautilus* quickly returned to the surface and started firing again. The diving, surfacing, and firing went on all day. At one point, the *Nautilus* came under fire from a Japanese gunboat in a nearby lagoon. The submarine's gun roared back at the gunboat and sank it.

Another highly effective weapon used against enemy shipping was the lightweight PT-boat. The wooden-hulled PTs raced to within a few hundred yards of their target before launching torpedos. PT crewmen referred to this as "throwing fish."

That night the outnumbered Marine raiders scrambled into their boats. A heavy surf had blown up and many of the raiders drowned while trying to reach their submarines. Only a handful made it. Six Marines were captured on Makin; the Japanese beheaded them.

Sinking the Japanese Empire

America was paying a heavy price for victory in the Pacific, but the cost of the war for Japan was even higher and increasing every day. Slowly but surely, the U.S. submarine offensive was sinking the Japanese merchant fleet and squeezing off the flow of oil and raw materials to the Home Islands. During four years of war, American submarines sent more than 1,100 Japanese merchant vessels to the bottom for a total of 5,320,094 gross tons of Japanese shipping sunk. The U.S. subs also downed more than 200 warships. By contrast, the Japanese managed to sink only forty-five American submarines.

Like a nest of hornets waiting to swarm over the enemy, a squadron of PT-boats gathers in a South Pacific lagoon.

Land-based warplanes sometimes caught enemy convoys out in the open with devastating results. During the Battle of the Bismark Sea, U.S. bombers wiped out a 22-ship convoy, sending 15,000 Japanese troops to the bottom with their transports. A B-25 attacks an enemy destroyer. Note the bomb and the Japanese sailors diving for cover.

By comparison with the Germans, who lost hundreds of U-boats to depth charges in the Atlantic, American submarine losses in the Pacific were relatively light. They faced less opposition from convoy escorts, and as a result, their voracious appetite for commercial shipping raged virtually unchecked throughout the war. The Japanese never developed an effective submarine defense.

By 1945, Japan had been almost totally cut off from the rich resources of Southeast Asia and even from nearby ports in Korea and China. Oil deliveries from the Dutch East Indies, the lifeblood of the Japanese military, had been slowed to a trickle. Fuel deliveries dropped so low that the Japanese could no longer train carrier pilots. By the time the Battle of the Philippines began, the oil-starved Imperial Navy was too weak to stop the Americans.

Chapter Six

Normandy: A Bridge to Victory

The invasion of Normandy, which began on June 6, 1944, was one of the most colossal events in human history. Nothing comparable to it has occurred since Classical times. On the night of June 5–6, 2,727 vessels of the United States, British, and Canadian navies and remnants of the French, Dutch, Polish, and Greek navies crossed the English Channel undetected. At dawn they started four British and three American divisions toward the shore in successive assault waves. By noon a beachhead had been established. Within a month the U.S. Navy would have landed the one-*millionth* American soldier on French soil.

Luck and weather played important roles in the invasion. But the key to its success was precise timing and close cooperation between the various Allied navies. The Allies had not always worked so well together. The United States entered the war two years after it began. Relatively speaking, the U.S. Navy was the new boy in a school of jaw-jarring knockout blows, while Britain's Royal Navy was the experienced old boy. Consequently, the British set the drum-beat for battle in the Atlantic and the Mediterranean while the U.S. called the tune in the Pacific.

Both navies were fighting a two-ocean war but neither had enough ships and men to do so alone. Early on, the two navies began to squabble over who would do what and who would help whom. The stage was set early in 1942 for

Storming the beaches at Normandy.

the Allies' two-ocean rivalry, as they sought to defeat their common enemies. Allied political leaders agreed that victory in Europe would be the first priority. But this "Europe first" approach did not sit well with some American military leaders who were eager to punish Japan for Pearl Harbor.

What is more, if the liberation of Europe were to be the first priority, U.S. leaders wanted to get on with the job, finish it, and turn their attention to the defeat of Japan. But the British were not so anxious to mount a massive invasion of Europe. The British preferred to harass the enemy with deftly executed raids conducted while mass bombings were demoralizing the enemy's civilian population. Perhaps Hitler would be overthrown by the Germans themselves. When and if an invasion became necessary, the British wanted to avoid the heavily fortified coasts of France and Holland. Instead, they suggested an attack on Europe's "soft underbelly"—the Mediterranean region.

The first major Allied invasion in the west came in 1942 in North Africa. The USS *Massachusetts* during a lull in the fighting at Casablanca where she dueled with the *Jean Bart*, eventually silencing the unfinished French battleship.

Chapter Six • NORMANDY: A Bridge to Victory

The Allies were unsure if French forces in North Africa would fight back. They did. A torpedo blasted this enormous hole in the destroyer *Hambleton* off the Moroccan coast.

The wrangling subsided after Operation Torch, the invasion of North Africa. This struggle against Rommel's Panzers pulled American forces into the British-dominated Mediterranean, where the two militaries found they could work well together after all. Strategists soon reached a compromise: The Allies would invade Europe through *both* its soft underbelly and the coast of France. The march toward victory in Europe had begun, and as it turned out, Normandy would be the key bridge that had to be crossed along the way.

Texas Stands with Britain

While strategists argued in London and Washington, Seaman First Class Leander Haakonson from Sauk Rapids, Minnesota, stood convoy duty in the North Atlantic aboard the battleship USS *Texas*. When it came to cooperation with the British, the *Texas* was a veteran. The venerable battlewagon had served with the Royal Navy during World War I. No stranger to France, it had escorted President Woodrow Wilson to the Paris Peace Conference in 1918. Since the autumn of 1939, the *Texas* had fought alongside the Royal Navy as part of the so-called "Neutrality Patrol." Officially, the Neutrality Patrol was intended to keep war out of the Western Hemisphere. In reality, it provided a shadow escort for convoys bound from Eastern Canada to Great Britain.

Heavy naval bombardment paved the way for troop landings. Major General George Patton heads for shore at Casablanca.

While the British struggled to hold back the Axis in Europe, the Great Depression lingered on in America, a state of affairs that left young men such as Haakonson few opportunities other than military service. In the spring of 1941 he was working with a survey crew in a Civilian Conservation Corps camp at Park Rapids, Minnesota. Haakonson's older brother decided to join the military and it seemed like a good idea. They signed up together and on Dec. 7, 1941, Haakonson was already aboard the *Texas*. When the dramatic news of that day reached him, his ship was anchored in Casco Bay, Maine, to allow the crew rest and recreation after a tiring stretch of escort duty out of Newfoundland. With the U.S. officially in the war, the *Texas* returned to the convoys.

In the fall of 1942, the *Texas* became part of Operation Torch, the North African invasion which began at Casablanca. Her 14-inch guns provided fire support for troops on shore. Except for the invasion of Guadalcanal, Operation Torch was the first amphibious assault the U.S. Navy had undertaken in forty-five years. It certainly was one of the boldest. Untested troops were put on transports at Norfolk, Virginia, and sent across the Atlantic while Navy picket boats scouted for U-boats.

Off North Africa they rendezvoused with a Royal Navy convoy and on November 8, the Anglo-American force went ashore in French Morocco. French land and naval forces in North Africa were loyal to France's Vichy government, which in turn was in league with the Axis. They put up a stiff but sporadic resistance. The *Texas* stood offshore with other ships of the combined fleet lobbing shells to clear a path for advancing Allied troops. The French had no long-range guns. The only return fire came from the *Jean Bart*, a French battleship still under construction and tied up alongside a dock at Casablanca. Although she fought bravely for a time, armor-piercing shells from U.S. ships soon silenced her.

With Morocco safely in Allied hands and Rommel's tanks being forced steadily back through the African sands, the *Texas* resumed convoy escort duty.

In preparation for the invasion of Europe, the Allies built up mountains of supplies in the British Isles. A jeep and its driver go for a ride.

The buildup of Allied forces in the British Isles was accelerating. Britain had become one vast staging area. Harbors were crammed with warships and merchant vessels. On shore millions of tons of supplies and war machinery were camouflaged from aerial observation by the Luftwaffe and hidden from the curious on land. Only a handful of American and British servicemen were privy to the specifics, but they all sensed that a climactic battle was approaching.

The monumental process of unleashing Operation Neptune Overlord—the Allied assault on Normandy—was set in motion stealthily. For many, it began in the darkness. Battle-ready British, Canadian, and American soldiers began their trek to embarkation points. The sound of tramping boots echoed in the night through the silent streets of blacked-out communities. An occasional softly spoken "God bless you" came from doorways. Not a whisper about the troop movements got beyond the English coastal villages. German intelligence never

Sergeant Miles Davis King carries a 20mm gun magazine during landing preparations.

Chapter Six • NORMANDY: A Bridge to Victory

learned the invasion date, the actual numbers of troops concentrated in Great Britain, or even that the invasion would come at Normandy. When Neptune Overlord began, there were 1,627,000 American troops in Great Britain. Aboard ships in the harbors were 52,889 American sailors and 112,824 Royal Navy sailors. Belfast Lough in Ireland was used to relieve the crowding in English, Scottish, and Welsh ports. Keeping secret an operation of such size surely ranks among the war's most astounding feats.

When the date set for the invasion arrived, Britain's highly unpredictable weather refused to cooperate. The attack was to begin on June 5, 1942, but on that day a fierce storm swept the English Channel. The overall commander of the operation was General Dwight David Eisenhower, and he decided to put off the assault for one day—no more. Otherwise it would be two weeks before the tides again favored a landing in France. The element of surprise was crucial, and the Allies could not risk losing it.

On the night of June 5, the largest invasion fleet in history headed for France, while overhead air transports began to ferry paratroopers across the channel for night drops behind enemy lines. Even with all this activity underway, the Germans on the far shore remained ignorant of Allied movements and intentions. German gunboat patrols along the French coast had been suspended. Their commander thought the weather too rough for patrol duty or an Allied invasion. The Luftwaffe had been flying, but its pilots had not seen anything they felt worth reporting. The powerful lamp in Normandy's Cape Barfleur Lighthouse kept burning—a symbolic invitation to the attackers.

Before dawn, right on schedule, thousands of vessels stood at their assigned stations off Normandy. They had arrived without collision, in spite of a tossing sea. Troops mustered on deck and began to climb down into landing craft.

For the Germans, a long strategic guessing game was about to end. As the Americans had wondered where the Japanese would strike in the Pacific, the Germans had wondered where the Allies would strike in Europe. On June 6, they found out. Shortly after 3:00 A.M., German radar technicians looked into their screens and saw blips—lots of them. Shore batteries were alerted, but they did not start shooting until first light.

A Chaplain on the Bridge

Just before dawn, the sky to the southeast of the battleship *Texas* lit up as Allied aircraft bombed the coast. It was a fireworks display such as Lieutenant (j.g.) C. LeGrande Moody had never seen before or since. Moody was the battleship's chaplain, and he was on the bridge describing the action over the ship's internal public address system. His parka was zipped up against the cold. A light fog hovered over the sea.

Back when the *Texas* was on convoy duty, Moody had begun reading weather forecasts and news items to the men to help break the tension and tedium of Atlantic crossings. The captain liked the idea and thought it good for morale. During Operation Torch, the skipper asked Moody to use the public

European theater commander Dwight David Eisenhower gives paratroopers their D-Day orders: "Full victory—nothing else."

address system to describe the battle for the crew, most of whom served below decks. When he was not performing other duties, and when activity on the bridge allowed, Moody gave the crew a running account of what he saw.

While still in high school in Dillon, South Carolina, Moody had joined the National Guard. A two-week encampment manning shore batteries on mosquito-infested Sullivan Island off Charleston convinced him that he wanted no part of Army life. If there was to be a war, he would prefer to spend it at sea. By the time the war started, Moody was studying at Yale Divinity School in New Haven, Connecticut. He and another divinity student wanted to join the Navy, but their recruiter told them to finish divinity school and come back. The Navy needed chaplains, so they finished at Yale and then joined up. After Chaplains School in Norfolk, Virginia, Moody reported aboard the *Texas* on September 3, 1942.

Chapter Six • NORMANDY: A Bridge to Victory 91

Now, nearly two years later, Moody stood on a wing of the bridge as the *Texas* and other battleships pounded Omaha Beach. In the predawn light, troop-laden landing craft began heading shoreward, and the ship's big guns opened up with increased fury. Their concussion split Moody's parka.

Down in Turret No. 2, Haakonson and his mates worked with a steady, rapid rhythm, as the 14-inch guns hurled their projectiles. Every time the guns went off the ship would roll. Haakonson's gun crew received their ammunition from below decks where Seaman First Class H. Robert Riley, Jr., helped pass 14-inch ammunition from the magazines to the gun hoists. Born in Indiana, he had been reared in Hamburg, New York. Like the ship's chaplain, he had joined the Navy in 1942.

The guns kept firing until 6:30 A.M., when the naval bombardment ceased. The first wave of troops was approaching the beach. The landing craft were going in abreast, wave after wave of them. Some were getting hit and capsizing. Others were simply blown out of the water. Then the Germans opened up on the beach with everything they had. The gunners on the ships could not fire back for fear of killing the men on the beach.

Infantrymen hit the beach running, automatic weapons fire scything through them as they ran toward the dirt road that led to Vierville. By the time the sur-

One of the heaviest naval bombardments in history preceded the Normandy landings. A U.S. battleship fires her 16-inch guns.

vivors of the first waves reached the cover of the seawall, so many company officers had been killed or wounded that the infantrymen did not know what to do next. More waves of landing craft were rolling in behind them, crowding the beach with troops who had no cover at all and made easy targets for the Germans. The Allies were pinned down, in danger of being slaughtered.

By 8:00 A.M., more than an hour after the first wave had hit the beach, no one had moved inland from the American sector. To the east the British had not done much better. At 8:30 A.M. the beach master halted further landings until the jumble ashore could be sorted out. Obstacles and debris had to be cleared out of the way. Braving intense German fire, Navy and Army underwater demolition teams started blasting additional landing craft channels through the beach obstacles. They worked in desperate haste, fighting against both the Germans and a

At Cherbourg, the battleship *Texas* locked horns with a battery of huge German railroad guns. Here the *Texas* carries a load of German and Italian prisoners of war. Notice seasick prisoners sprawled on the deck.

Chapter Six • NORMANDY: A Bridge to Victory

While naval forces landed more and more supplies in Normandy, the Army pushed further and further inland. A French partisan and an American officer fight side by side on a city street.

rising tide. Five wide channels and three partial ones were cleared, but at a high price. Most members of the demolition teams were killed. Meanwhile, sailors had been steering their landing craft evasively in the choppy water offshore, waiting for an opportunity to head in with troops and supplies. Two Navy reservists saw an opening and headed for it. Their example was followed by others and the momentum of the assault was regained.

Badly needed Army artillery had still not made it ashore, so the Navy took up the slack with 5-inch guns. Much of the time they were firing blind. Most of the sailors who went ashore with the infantry to direct fire from the ships had been killed or wounded. Destroyers, their guns blazing, rushed shoreward, risking grounding, to get a direct line of fire on the enemy. German artillerymen were using a church steeple on a hilltop to spot fire on their attackers. The guns of the *Texas* toppled it.

Der Führer himself posing in Paris on June 23, 1940—better times for the Third Reich. Four years later, the Normandy landings set the stage for the liberation of Paris.

Chapter Six • NORMANDY: A Bridge to Victory 95

By August, 1944—three months after D-Day—U.S. soldiers could get an up-close view of the Eiffel Tower.

As D-Day wore on, wounded Army Rangers were brought to the battleship's sick bay and Moody went below to minister to the wounded and dying. The blood on the sick bay floor made it difficult for him to keep his footing.

Eventually, having fired all its ammunition, the *Texas* sailed to Plymouth for more. When it returned to the Normandy coast, Anglo-American forces were fighting in the French countryside. Although extraordinarily bloody, the D-Day landings had been a success.

For the next two weeks, men and supplies steadily poured into the landing zone. By the end of the day on June 18, the U.S. Navy had put ashore 314,514 American troops, 41,000 vehicles, and 16,000 tons of supplies. In the British sector, the Royal Navy had landed 314,547 troops, 54,000 vehicles, and 102,000 tons of supplies. Both navies had built artificial breakwaters, some of them by sinking American-built Liberty ships.

Many miles inland, the Germans flung division after division at the invaders trying to drive them back into the sea. They were not succeeding, but nature was about to land a blow of its own on the Allies. In the early morning of June 19, the worst storm in forty years swept the Channel. It lasted two days and left debris-littered beaches and ruined breakwaters in its wake.

The Allied command realized that their advance on the port of Cherbourg must be speeded up. Without a secure port, the campaign might still fail. On June 25, the American and British ships started shelling German positions around Cherbourg. During the operation, the *Texas*, the battleship *Arkansas*, and several destroyers found themselves fighting a battery of 11-inch guns east of the city. The Germans had mounted the guns on railway cars and concealed them in tunnels. They would wheel out to fire and then roll back into the safety of the tunnels.

Trying to lob shells into the mouths of the tunnels, the *Texas* fired its big guns every 35 seconds. Haakonson and his crew worked quickly and with precision, but their arms were getting weak from wrestling the heavy shells and the 104-pound powder bags into place. In the conning tower gunnery officers were doing their mathematical best to put the guns on target. For the Germans, the battleship was an easy target and they were firing back. Below decks Riley could hear the rattle of shrapnel against the side of the hull. Projectiles from the huge railroad guns were coming closer and closer to the *Texas*.

Realizing they were under fire, the ship's crew discovered reserves of energy they never knew they possessed. Haakonson and his mates loaded and reloaded, loaded and reloaded. Each time the breech slammed home, they leaped onto the six-inch platforms inside the turret, turned their feet sideways, and gripped the grab-rails with their hands as the big guns recoiled backward 54 inches. As the guns began their forward slide, the gun crews reloaded them once again.

The steel face and sides of Turret No. 2 were 16 inches thick, the back about 7 inches thick, and the top 5 inches thick. The only openings in its armament were viewing slits, a fact that may have saved the lives of Haakonson and his crew. A German 280mm armor-piercing shell hit the conning tower above the turret and was deflected upward into the bridge, where it exploded. The concussion in the turret made the gunners' eyeballs roll. Paint peeled off the overhead and the bulkheads. The gun crew thought the turret had been hit, but they kept loading.

In the conning tower, one of the junior gunnery officers had taken over from the gun boss. When the shell hit, he had been looking through a periscope. He was knocked out and remained in a daze for about a week. Chaplain Moody had been standing on the bridge wing when the shell hit. A piece of shrapnel put a crease in his steel helmet; he was in shock, but miraculously unhurt. The helmsman, whom Moody had been talking with seconds earlier, had his hand blown off. Moody held a pressure point in the helmsman's arm to keep him from bleeding to death. Other sailors lay in the wreckage, some with legs blown off from the upward explosion. The captain and the navigation officer, who had rushed in from the chart room, cleared the bridge and got the wounded to sick bay. Another shell ripped through the hull about 60 feet back from the port bow and above the waterline. It had bounced off the water and come in sideways, breaking its firing pin as it came through the hull. Sailors secured the wildly rolling shell with mattresses.

Cherbourg was surrendered to the Allies the following day. Haakonson recalled a Royal Navy battleship steaming by to salute USS *Texas* for a job well done. Shells from the German railroad guns had straddled the American battlewagon thirty-five times.

Lieutenant Moody received a commendation for aiding the wounded on the bridge. Later in the war, he served as a chaplain on Guam. He left the Navy in 1947, returned to South Carolina, and became a minister in the United Methodist Church. Many years later, Moody visited the American cemetery at Normandy... and wept as he read the markers.

Chapter Seven

LEYTE GULF: The Fight for the Philippines

By 1944, a death knell for the Japanese Imperial Navy had begun to toll in the Pacific. Japan's hope for a quick victory before America's mass production industries could be retooled for all-out war had been dashed at Midway. In Europe the tide of war had turned in favor of the Allies and the U.S. Navy began to shift large numbers of its ships from the Atlantic to the Pacific theater. Unrestricted submarine warfare had slowed to a trickle the flow of oil to the home islands, further crippling the Japanese fleet. But the Imperial Navy had one last blast of fury left in it, and this was unleashed in October, 1944, at the Battle of Leyte Gulf.

Triggered by the United States' invasion of the Japanese-held Philippine Islands, the bitterly fought battle was actually a series of four widely separated but major actions—on the Sibuyan Sea, in Surigao Strait, near Cape Enagano, and off Samar. The Japanese battle plan was a bold one. They would fling at the Americans three large fleets comprised of nearly every Japanese warship still afloat and serviceable. To get them all into action at once meant draining to the bottom the country's remaining stocks of fuel oil. Approaching from three different directions, the fleets would attempt to converge on the American fighting ships and transports in the Philippines. The roar and mayhem of history's largest and most complex naval battle lasted four days.

A line of U.S. warships heads for the Philippines. The battleship *Pennsylvania* leads.

Relying on fast carriers and air power, U.S. forces continued to advance through the Pacific.

The Japanese took an incredible beating. The U.S. fleet sank dozens of enemy warships including several carriers. Often Imperial Navy pilots returned to their carriers and found them aflame and sinking. Sometimes their carriers were nowhere to be seen at all, having already slipped beneath the waves, stranding their pilots in the air with their planes running out of fuel. Poignantly, some Japanese pilots actually tried to land on American carriers. Lieutenant Commander Peter Black saw an enemy pilot attempt to land on his escort carrier, the *Marcus Island*. "The flight deck officer waved him off," Black recalls. "I guess he must have crashed into the sea."

When the battle of Leyte Gulf was over, the Japanese Imperial Navy had ceased to exist as an effective fighting force.

Aboard the *Alabama*

Racing from one critical assignment to another amid the confusion of Leyte was a relatively new player in the Pacific war, the fast battleship USS *Alabama*. Her 16-inch guns supported American troops ashore, and her antiaircraft batteries defended U.S. carriers from Japanese air strikes.

The 680-foot long, 35,000-displacement-ton *Alabama* was commissioned at Portsmouth, Virginia, on August 16, 1942, nearly two years after John Brown of Edwight, West Virginia, joined the Navy. He had just graduated from high school in nearby Beckley and for a long time had it in mind to join the Navy. Brown figured the Navy would keep him out of the coal mines, and that it did.

When the Japanese attacked Pearl Harbor, Brown was serving in the Navy Honor Guard in Washington, D.C. Later he was assigned to the staff of Admiral Ernest J. King, Chief of Naval Operations. Still a seaman, Brown was placed on the precommissioning detail for the *Alabama*. He served on the big ship for the rest of the war.

The *Alabama* began its fighting career in the Atlantic, but in mid-1943, she was sent to the Pacific. She arrived just as the Guadalcanal fighting was winding

These exhausted Marines have just helped take the key island of Eniwetock from its determined Japanese defenders.

down and the American island-hopping campaign across the Pacific was beginning in earnest. The *Alabama*'s big guns first boomed in anger in the Gilbert and Marshall Islands. Usually, they were employed to blast a path for Marines through island defenses.

By now Brown was Turret Captain First Class in charge of the after-turret housing three 16-inch guns, each capable of firing a shell weighing as much as an automobile. The battleship's six other 16-inch guns were housed, three each, in the vessel's two forward turrets. The swiveling, 21-ton turrets in which the guns were raised or lowered as they were swung into firing position concealed a forest of hoists running down to powder magazines and shell decks inside the ship. Shells and powder were moved by electrically powered hydraulic mechanisms and it was Brown's job to see that all the machinery was kept in working order.

Once an island was taken, it usually became an air base, preparing the way for yet another step toward the Philippines and Japan. A Marine leads a taxiing U.S. bomber on Eniwetock.

Chapter Seven • LEYTE GULF: The Fight for the Philippines   **103**

When the U.S. invasion of the Philippines began in October, 1944, the Japanese attacked with all their remaining naval might. The U.S. fleet was waiting for them and PT-boats were the first to go in against the enemy. An alert PT marksman is ready for action.

The after turret had a full-time crew of twenty men, but during combat, the crew was increased to more than a hundred. It took lots of muscle to load the hoists with powder and shells for the hungry guns aloft. There was no air-conditioning and the powder crews had to be rotated to keep them from getting drunk on the ether fumes that swirled around them as they opened canisters of smokeless powder. They were rotated as soon as they became tipsy, and when their heads cleared, they went back to work in the magazines.

Behind a Foot of Steel

Three decks below the turrets, approximately in the ship's center and protected by its armored hull, was the main battle control center. Here officers and sailors directed the aiming of guns and then fired them electrically. Inside each

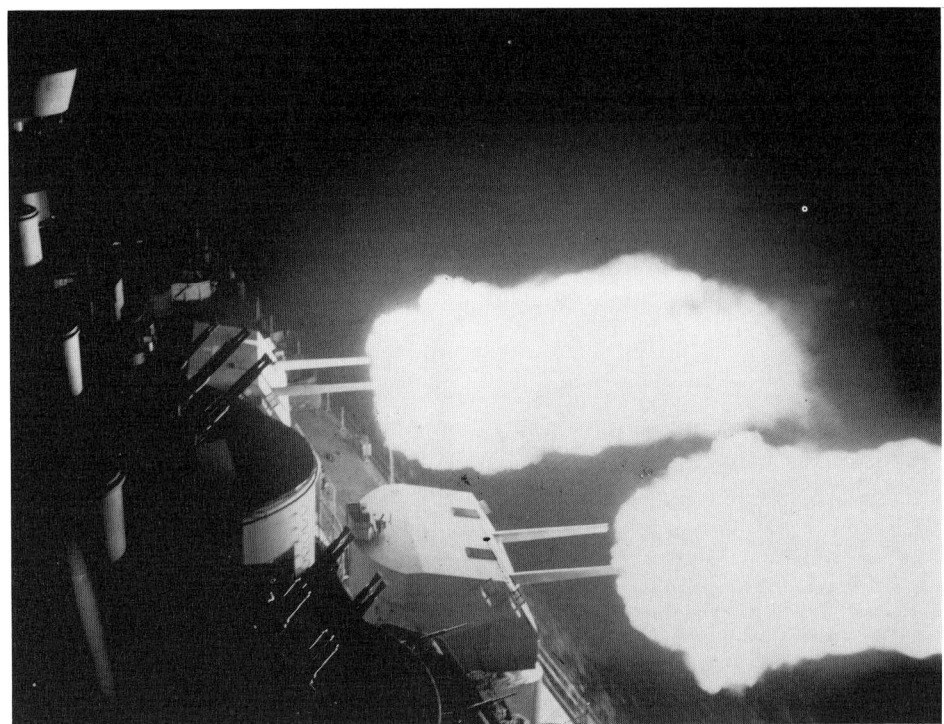

In a night action on October 24, the U.S. Seventh Fleet wiped out a large Japanese flotilla. Five-inch guns blaze away in the darkness.

turret an officer duplicated the firing plots of the main battle control center. As the 2,700-pound projectiles and 540 pounds of powder that made up each round whirred up the hoists, the men in the turret tugged and wrestled them into the guns. Then they jumped aside to escape the recoil. Once the system was in full operation, it worked as efficiently as one of the clip-fed M-1 rifles used by soldiers on shore. A good turret crew could get a round off every 20 seconds.

The guns were 68 feet long and their breeches two feet thick. The instant the breech was opened to insert another round, air jets from a compressor system blew all the smoke from the barrel. It was quite noisy inside the turret, and heat built up from the hydraulic system and the huge motors that were used to operate it. The men inside the turret could not see outside. But they could hear the *Alabama*'s antiaircraft slamming round after round at attacking Japanese aircraft. They could hear the sound of the battleship's engine and turbines working beneath them. They heard and felt the throaty scream of the propeller coming clear of the water in heavy seas, its spin shaking the ship from stem to stern.

The steady, rapid pace inside the turret never let up. Outside the big guns belched flames at the sky. Fire danced from their muzzles like a dragon's tongue. "We were engrossed in what we were doing," said Brown. "I never heard anyone bitch or complain. You were out there to do the best you could. The whole country was in uniform, and they wanted to get the job over and go home. We were no different."

Chapter Seven • LEYTE GULF: The Fight for the Philippines

On October 25, a powerful Imperial Navy fleet led by the massive battleship *Yamato* slipped through a narrow strait and descended on several lightly defended U.S. carriers. To protect the carriers and the U.S. beachhead beyond, a small fleet of American destroyers launched a desperate counterattack. All but a few of the destroyers were sunk or severely damaged, but the Japanese withdrew. This watercolor by Commander Dwight Shepler depicts the action off Samar.

U.S. carrier planes mercilessly pounded the Japanese. An Imperial Navy carrier under attack north of the Philippines.

Exhausted Navy pilots during the assault on the Luzon.

Although the gunners could not see the fighting, apprehension built up in the turrets and the gun mounts as a battle unfolded. But there was also a relative sense of security in serving on a big ship such as the *Alabama* with a foot or more of steel between the gunners and the enemy.

Men in the turrets also had responsibility for the antiaircraft guns that were manned round-the-clock. Brown was the controlling operator for one of *Alabama*'s twin 5-inch gun mounts used for antiaircraft fire. There were ten of these mounts on the battleship. He was in the mount more than he was in the turret since the battleship's biggest guns were fired only on those occasions when their annihilating knockout punch was needed.

When he left the Philippines in 1942, General Douglas MacArthur said "I shall return." Two and a half years later he did.

Carrier task forces were frequently under air attack by Japanese dive bombers and torpedo planes. The gun mounts were operated in much the same manner as the big turrets. In the plotting room the speed, altitude, and range of attacking aircraft were tracked on radar before they could be seen by the men on deck. The calculations were transmitted to the gunnery department, which fired the 5-inch guns electrically. Inside the sealed gun mounts, Brown and his crews would set the fuses on the 54-pound shells to determine how far out and how high up they would explode. The guns blasted away relentlessly at the incoming Japanese planes while they struggled to maneuver through the shifting patterns of exploding metal that Brown and his shipmates hurled at them.

"You could kick the rounds out from the mounts a hell of a lot faster than you could from the turrets," said Brown. "We needed only about five seconds [to prepare the gun for the next round]." The powder and projectiles came up from below on hoists, just as in the turrets. A good crew could reload the 5-inch rounds in three or four seconds.

Although the 5-inch guns fired rapidly, their aim was carefully controlled, and Japanese pilots seldom penetrated the curtain of flak thrown up over the ship. When they did, the smaller 20 and 40 millimeter antiaircraft guns took over. Their gunners tracked the incoming aircraft visually through their sights. "There was a hell of a lot of firing," said Brown. "During one fight, two Japanese aircraft were splashed right alongside *Alabama*. It was the closest we came to being hit during the [entire] war."

Brown fought in action after action in campaigns for the Marshalls, the Gilberts, the Marianas, Okinawa, Formosa, and Hollandia. Nearly all of his fighting time was spent firing the 5-inch guns to protect American carriers. The older battleships, including ones that had been refloated after Pearl Harbor, were used primarily for shore bombardment since they were too slow for carrier escort duty. Leyte was just another operation for Brown, who had been keeping *Alabama*'s guns firing since she arrived in the Pacific. "Philippine Sea, Leyte Gulf, they all seemed about the same to me," said Brown.

Brown is one of only a few U.S. Navy sailors who also served in the Army. He got out of the Navy in 1946. When he tried to re-enlist three years later, there was no room for him in the peacetime Navy. So Brown joined the Army. In 1950 he was a first sergeant with the First U.S. Infantry Division fighting in Korea. The mud, the cold, the heat, the face-to-face combat, and the fear altered his perspective of war. He received a battlefield commission in Korea, remained in the Army, and also fought in Vietnam. After 22 years he retired as a lieutenant colonel. Brown said that if he had to do it over again he would have spent all of his time in the Navy. "You could always get a cup of coffee in the Navy or lie down and take a break between fights," he noted. "On a battleship you had leisure hours and you felt comfortable. You never faced the same fear an infantryman faces."

Brown liked being on the *Alabama* so much that nowadays he is back on board—as director of Battleship Memorial Park in Mobile, where the retired battleship is by far the biggest attraction.

Chapter Eight

OKINAWA: Hell Fighters

Its code name was Operation Iceberg. But there was nothing cold about it. The landing on Okinawa was the last amphibious operation of the war and also one of the most daring and complex. Like Guadalcanal it was tough, long, and bitter—just more so. It was the last-ditch stand of the Japanese Empire, and it was, practically speaking, the last leg in the long march across the Pacific.

The taking of Okinawa was the second step of a two-step maneuver. Iwo Jima had been the first step. The goal, of course, was to deliver a knockout blow to Japan. The Battle of Okinawa began for the Navy in March of 1945, just as fighting was winding down on Iwo Jima. Before it was over, it would cost the Navy 4,900 sailors killed or missing in action and more than 4,800 wounded. Thirty-four naval vessels would be sunk and 368 damaged. Ashore, the Tenth Army would grimly tally its losses as 7,613 killed or missing in action and 31,800 wounded.

Many of the naval losses could be chalked up to kamikaze ("divine wind") attacks by Japanese pilots who steered their own bomb-laden airplanes into U.S. ships. At Okinawa, the Japanese launched more than 3,000 individual kamikaze attacks. The constant threat of the kamikazes kept crews tense and sleepless. Sleep became as precious for American sailors as a stateside liberty had once been. But this was a fight that had to be fought.

Kamikaze bomber dives on the carrier *Hornet*. A watercolor by Commander Dwight Shepler.

The last major step on the road to victory in the Pacific came at Okinawa. A U.S. battleship shells the enemy as landing craft head for the beach.

Island bases were needed for a final assault on Japan. Tokyo lay at one end of a triangle formed by Saipan and Taiwan (Formosa) from which B-29 Superforts could be sent on missions of devastation. The United States had already wrested Saipan from the Japanese. But Japan still occupied Taiwan and defenses there were formidable. Rural but heavily populated, Okinawa lay at the outer edge of Japan's Inland Sea, and it was crucial. By replacing Taiwan, Okinawa was to become the missing point in the triangle.

Iwo Jima was needed to provide a temporary emergency landing strip for B-29s flying the Saipan—Tokyo—Okinawa triangle, and it was secured first. The fighting at Iwo Jima was tough, but U.S. military planners thought Okinawa could be taken more easily. They were wrong. Japan was determined to make the Americans pay dearly for their strategic real estate. They had ringed and crisscrossed both islands with stout, intricate defenses.

Chapter Eight • OKINAWA: Hell Fighters

B-29 Superforts were already raining incendiary bombs on major Japanese cities. In a single night of air strikes, 250,000 homes were destroyed and 83,793 people killed. With their Home Islands under attack, Japan's warriors fought with a new vengeance. Driven from Iwo Jima's steaming and fetid jungle, Japanese infantrymen fell back to carefully prepared and concealed bunkers and carried on the struggle. Marines were forced to take the island foot by bloody foot.

On Okinawa, Army infantrymen repeated the same deadly, exhausting advance. The Tenth Army started going ashore on Okinawa on April 1, 1945, Easter Sunday. The British Royal Navy's Pacific fleet, strengthened with warships freed from duty in the Atlantic, had already hit Japanese airfields on Sakashima Gunto, an island 230 miles away, and started intercepting forays by Japanese aircraft from Taiwan. The preemptive air strikes launched from Royal Navy carriers were intended to knock the stuffing out of Japan's ability to defend Okinawa from the air.

The steel decks of Royal Navy carriers frustrated kamikaze counterattacks. Unlike the wooden flight decks of American flattops, those of British carriers

Diagram of a 16-inch gun turret on a battleship.

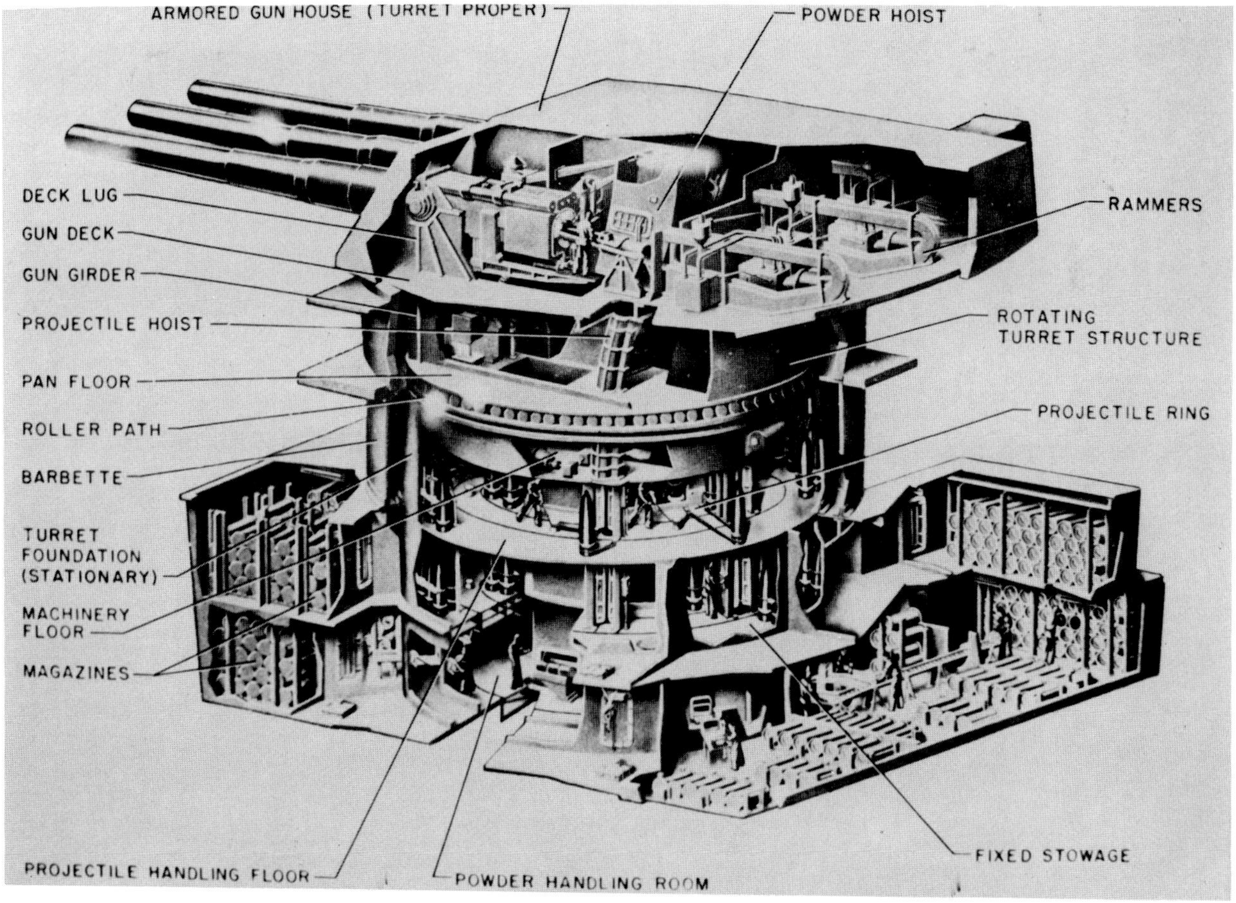

The Japanese struck back against overpowering Allied naval strength with a fearsome weapon, the Kamikaze or suicide bomber. A Kamikaze strikes the communications tower before crashing into the deck of the USS *Franklin*.

Fire in a 5-inch gun mount aboard the often wounded carrier *Franklin*.

Chapter Eight • OKINAWA: Hell Fighters

The Kamikazes took a heavy toll. Burial at sea after a suicide attack on the carrier *Intrepid*.

crumpled diving kamikazes into piles of debris that could be shoved over the side. To save weight and fuel, U.S. carrier designers had given American carriers wooden decks. This gave them more speed and range, but made them vulnerable to kamikaze attack. For this reason, the U.S. Navy sheltered its carriers with a formidable armada of escort ships. Battleships were kept nearby to serve as anti-aircraft platforms and to shield the carriers from enemy planes.

While the British were decimating nearby Japanese air squadrons, American carriers struck Japanese military installations on Taiwan, in Indo-China and China, and on the Japanese mainland, destroying hundreds of aircraft. Helping screen the roving carriers was the 728-foot, 35,000-ton battleship *North Carolina*, known to her crew as the "Showboat." Able to slice through Pacific waves at just under 28 knots, she had already fought in twelve major engagements including Guadalcanal. At Okinawa, the *North Carolina*'s 16-inch gun turrets bombarded island defenses while her 5-inch guns splashed kamikazes and conventional warplanes trying to break up the invasion force.

Serving aboard the Showboat was Paul Wieser. While still in high school, Wieser had joined the Citizens Military Training Corps. He wanted to be a soldier, but he changed his mind when the Army took him on two weeks of maneuvers. Wieser was no camper. He did not like sleeping in the woods. He did not

Most Kamikaze bombers were conventional planes, but the Japanese built these aircraft especially for suicide missions. Heavy and barely maneuverable, they were little more than piloted bombs.

like crawling through grass. So, at the age of 17 and with his high school diploma in hand, he joined the Navy. Nine months later the Japanese attacked Pearl Harbor. When the *North Carolina* entered the Pacific in 1942, Wieser sailed with her.

At Guadalcanal Wieser was introduced to combat. As it does to most fighting men, the realization that people were trying to kill him came as a shock. It was a difficult notion to accept, but fighting back came naturally. Self-doubt evaporated with the first round he fired, and Wieser knew he would be okay. He knew he had a job to do. By the time he got to Okinawa, Wieser was a hardened veteran with several years of fighting behind him. He was also a Boatswain's Mate First Class and captain of a 5-inch gun mount.

The noise from *North Carolina*'s 16-inch guns was deafening as the camouflaged battleship bombarded Okinawa to "soften it up" for the invasion. At first the big guns belched their 2,700-pound projectiles at a part of the island away from the invasion zone. The misdirected fire was intended as a diversion, but the ploy did not work. Later the battleship shifted her fire to the landing zone. After the troops were ashore, the *North Carolina* alternated between providing support fire for troops and running escort for carriers launching air strikes on Japan.

Chapter Eight • OKINAWA: Hell Fighters

The air off Okinawa was constantly buzzing with kamikazes. It was blazing hot inside the 5-inch gun turrets as Wieser and his mates blasted the suicide planes out of the sky. And it was a noisy fight. The motors that powered the ammunition hoists and rammed home powder charges kept up a steady rumble. Reports of the guns, the roar of airplane engines, the impact of kamikazes disintegrating as they hit the water or screamed into another ship added to the din inside the turrets. The men loading the guns were forced to use sign language in order to communicate.

Throughout the battle, permanently assigned to beachhead duty, USS *Texas* fired her 14-inch guns in support of the slowly advancing infantry. Gunner's Mate Second Class Leander Haakonson, in the *Texas*'s No. 2 turret, was a veteran of the invasions of North Africa and Normandy. He described Okinawa as "hairy." Having air cover at Okinawa did not mean what it had meant at Normandy. The German Luftwaffe pilots had been gutsy, but the Japanese kamikaze pilots were overtly suicidal. Haakonson thought they were crazy.

During the long fight, *Texas* sailors remained at their general quarters stations for 54 consecutive days. Haakonson and his mates lived in turret No. 2, firing the guns. They ate K-rations when they could spare a few minutes. That was all they ate. They left the turret only to go to the head, one man at a time—and only twice a day. In the North Atlantic it had been cold inside the turret, but now it was miserably hot. The heavy work of feeding the 14-inch guns was done in temperatures of up to 120°F. When the temperature inside the turret dropped to 100° Haakonson thought it felt cool.

The battle station of Seaman First Class H. Robert Riley, Jr., was below, passing up ammunition for the 3-inch guns. When he heard the 40mm guns firing he knew kamikazes were approaching. When the 20mm guns started firing

Even the huge battleship *Yamato* was sent on a Kamikaze mission. Its tanks filled with only enough fuel to reach Okinawa, it took a desperate lunge at the Allied fleet. Carrier planes sank the massive warship while it was still far from its objective. The *Yamato* under air attack.

While the Navy absorbed blow after blow from Kamikazes, Allied soldiers fought for every yard taken from Okinawa's tenacious defenders. A wounded American private is evacuated.

After many weeks of hard fighting, Allied forces secured Okinawa. A U.S. Marine shares a canteen with a Japanese girl found in a cave on the island.

he knew they were getting closer. Then Riley began thinking of places to hide. But he kept passing the ammunition. It was hard, monotonous work, but below decks it was not so hot and from time to time the powder handlers could take a break.

Texas fired off so much ammunition during the battle for Okinawa, she had to be resupplied four times. The ship fired salvo after salvo at Japanese positions on shore, shot down one kamikaze, and helped splash three others. Together with the battleships USS *Arkansas* and USS *Nevada, Texas* bombarded the island before the invasion and then provided call-in fire support for the Army troops ashore.

Riley recalls the relief aboard *Texas* when the word was passed on April 7 that a Japanese strike force, intent on breaking up the beachhead, had been defeated. The Japanese force had been led by the *Yamato*, the world's largest battleship. If the last desperate sortie of the Japanese Imperial Navy had been successful, Riley and his mates were prepared to die defending the beachhead. Their desire was to finish the war and go home.

Yamato, the pride of the Japanese fleet, was sunk by a swarm of U.S. Navy carrier planes. Its loss had a powerful meaning for sailors on both sides of the war. *Yamato* was as graceful as she was immense. She was 826 feet long and displaced 72,908 tons. Her main battery of 18-inch guns could hurl 3,200-pound shells more than 22 miles, and she could cut through the water at nearly 28 knots. When *Yamato* sank, she took five centuries of battleship development and tradition with her. With the advent of the big fleet carriers, the battleship had lost it preeminent status as queen of the seas.

As the Battle of Okinawa neared its conclusion, the men of the *Texas* took a break on the beach. They had not been off the ship in months. Although the U.S. Navy had jettisoned its standard ration of grog during the Civil War, it sometimes found ways to wink at regulations for old times' sake. The official liberty party menu was lemonade and sandwiches, but before going ashore, the sailors could buy beer tickets. No more than three bottles of beer were allowed to any one sailor, but hard-drinking sailors found it easy to get around the limit: They simply had non-drinkers buy extra tickets for them.

The Final Days

With B-29s raining bombs on Japan and battleships shelling coastal installations within 40 miles of Tokyo, the Japanese military was in full retreat. Finally, the Navy issued heavy-weather clothing to its sailors and sent the fleet north. The Pacific Fleet would shiver in the North Pacific, out of harm's way, while the Army Air Force delivered the last crushing blows. The mushroom clouds that sprouted over Hiroshima and Nagasaki ended the war and ushered in a whole new and horrifying era of warfare.

On September 2, 1945, aboard USS *Missouri* anchored in Tokyo Bay, representatives of Japan's government surrendered. Soon after, the U.S. Navy began sending warships and sailors home.

Even after the fall of Okinawa, some Japanese leaders vowed to fight on, but when this mushroom cloud sprouted over Nagasaki on August 9, 1945, the war came to an end. Three days earlier, Hiroshima had been similarly devastated. Since more than 100,000 people—most of them civilians—were killed or injured in the Nagasaki explosion alone, it was not a glorious end to the war. But it was an end. When he had seen the world's first atomic explosion some weeks earlier in the New Mexico desert, nuclear scientist Robert Oppenheimer was reminded of words from the Hindu epic Bhagavad-Gita: "I am become Death, the shatterer of worlds." The same words might apply to war itself.

That fall Boatswain's Mate Wieser arrived in Boston aboard *North Carolina* and was reunited with his high school sweetheart. They had been married while he was on a liberty, but they had not seen each other in two years. Wieser got out of the Navy in 1946. He joined the Navy Reserve and was called to active duty during the Korean War.

The *Texas* became part of the Magic Carpet Fleet which carried troops home from the Pacific. She shuttled back and forth between Hawaii and California. When it was time for Gunner's Mate Haakonson to come home, he was taken aboard *Iowa*. It was a fast, modern battleship which might have had a chance in a duel with *Yamato*, but it was not to Haakonson's liking. He missed the feeling of family he had had on the old *Texas*. There were too many people on the *Iowa*—more than 3,500. The *Texas* had had a crew of only 1,700. Haakonson had loved battleships as he knew them. When he got out of the Navy he would miss the baked beans that were served family-style on the *Texas*. Haakonson was discharged in November 1945, returned to Minnesota, and got married, and eventually became a heavy equipment mechanic.

Seaman First Class Riley went to business school on the G.I. Bill, became an accountant, married, and moved to Florida, where he worked for a company that manufactured liquid oxygen for the space program.

Chapter Nine

GOING HOME: Back in the U.S. of A.

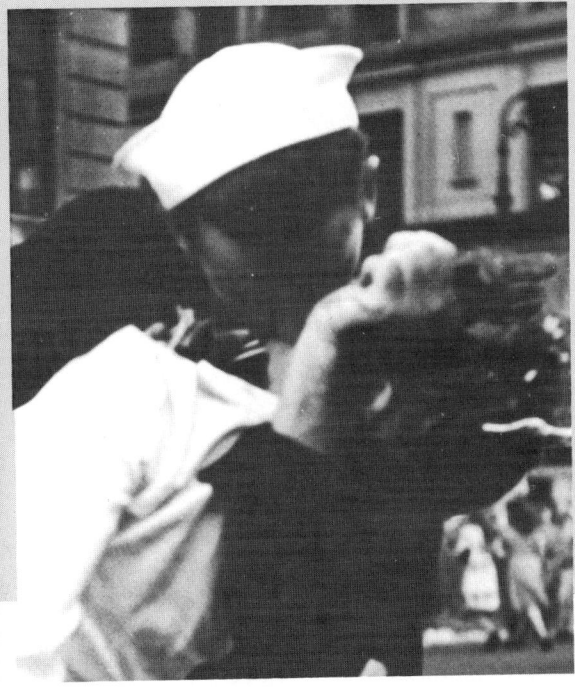

For each American sailor who survived the war, the experience of going home again was one of profound significance, something they would remember for the rest of their lives. They had done their duty. They had taken the enemy's worst and lived to tell about it. They had traveled to places with names most Americans could not even pronounce. And now they were back on home ground again. They had dreamed of this moment practically every night on the world's oceans and in overseas ports. And now it had come. Bathed in familiar sights and sounds and boisterously welcomed by familiar people, they were home. But the feelings they had now were not so familiar to them. Little by little most of them would come to realize that home would never be the same place again.

Good News on the *Nautilus*

Homecoming came earlier for Torpedoman Third Class McKinley than for most World War II sailors. While on a combat patrol at sea in 1943 he learned that he had passed his entrance examination to the Naval Academy. The good news was doubly surprising for McKinley since his first examination had been lost in the confusion following the attack on Pearl Harbor. His captain had made

An important message delivered in traditional Navy style: *The war is over!*

September 2, 1945. The Japanese delegation arrives aboard the battleship *Missouri* to sign surrender documents.

special arrangements for him to take the exam again, and McKinley had completed it on board the submarine while his shipmates watched and made comments. The *Nautilus* was outbound from Pearl Harbor on its way to intercept Japanese convoys when the good news came.

As one of only 100 Navy enlisted men who had passed the examination, McKinley took a lot of teasing from his shipmates. Of course, they were all happy for him, but perhaps they were also a little sad for themselves. "We all wanted to kill as many Japs as we could, but any one of us would have given almost anything to get back to the States," said McKinley.

The *Nautilus* dropped McKinley off at Midway. From there he would have to work his way back to the U.S. as best he could. He came ashore at Midway in his steaming shoes, the scuffed, comfortable ones he wore on patrol aboard *Nautilus*. There had not been time to change them. *Nautilus* had headed out of Pearl Harbor on what would have been McKinley's fourth combat patrol, the captain had diverted to Midway, and McKinley was told he was being dropped

Chapter Nine • GOING HOME: Back in the U.S. of A.

People had almost forgotten what it meant to live in peacetime. The world had begun its descent into war almost a decade earlier. Nazi Storm Troopers at Nuremberg in 1935.

off only as the black-hulled submarine slid towards the pier. McKinley had no idea things would happen so fast. He quickly packed his gear. He was going home. He was out of the war.

The torpedoman took up temporary quarters on a submarine tender for a few days and then another submarine returning from patrol was diverted to take McKinley back to Pearl Harbor. On Oahu he was sent to the Marine ammunition depot at Lua Lua Lei where he found out why the Marine raiders on the *Nautilus* had displayed such a liking for submarine chow. The food in the Marine mess at Lua Hua Lei was less than appetizing.

World War II united Americans as never before. Workers could laugh at a poster like this, but everyone understood that Mussolini, Tojo, and Hitler were not comic characters.

McKinley soon escaped the Marine Corps diet by hitching a ride on a battleship bound for California. Sleeping with only a single piece of canvas between him and a steel deck, McKinley often thought of the hammock, mattress, and pillow he had on the *Nevada*. No doubt they had been on the ship when it was torpedoed and sunk at Pearl Harbor. But McKinley was far less interested in his sleeping accommodations than he was in the fact that he was going home.

Through the Golden Gate

McKinley would soon realize it was easier to transit the Pacific in a submarine on combat patrol than it was to get across the United States. Civilian bus and train schedules were frequently scrambled by troop movements, and gasoline rationing made long-distance travel by car painstakingly slow. In San

People grumbled and complained, but most cooperated with rationing programs and willingly made material sacrifices to speed victory. For instance, movie star Rita Hayworth sacrificed her bumpers.

Francisco, McKinley found the harried yeomen at the Treasure Island receiving station awash in paperwork. There were too many sailors and not enough buses and trains to transport them. It would take at least two weeks before the yeomen could get McKinley on his way to Annapolis. In the meantime, McKinley would be allowed one liberty. Great! McKinley put in for a weekend liberty to see his parents in Southern California. Military bureaucrats denied the proposed destination because it was too far away, but McKinley was granted a restricted liberty anyway.

Servicemen overseas just wanted to get the war over and come home. A signpost on Leyte.

Being a sailor in wartime required constant vigilance. Lives depended on it.

Chapter Nine • GOING HOME: Back in the U.S. of A.

There were occasions for relaxation, but never for long. Sailors listening to a Victrola and enjoying a South Pacific beach party during a break in the fighting.

McKinley had not been home for three years. Most of that time had been spent in combat in the Pacific. Compared to the thousands of miles of ocean he had traversed, home was just down the road. Nothing essential to the war effort was being performed at the receiving station. "To hell with it," McKinley said to himself. "I'm going home."

Early one morning, he and another sailor began hitchhiking the 500 miles from San Francisco to Los Angeles. Getting rides was easy. The two sailors were in uniform, and during World War II most motorists felt it a duty to give servicemen rides. Even so, the two sailors moved very slowly toward their goal. Gasoline rationing required motorists to tread very lightly on their accelerators. Most of the cars they rode in crawled along at 35 miles per hour, and it took

Most of the time military food ranged from okay to not-so-good. Usually, sailors ate better than other servicemen, but Navy chow could never compare with home-cooked meals.

These sailors on Guadalcanal are obviously dreaming of Mom's cooking.

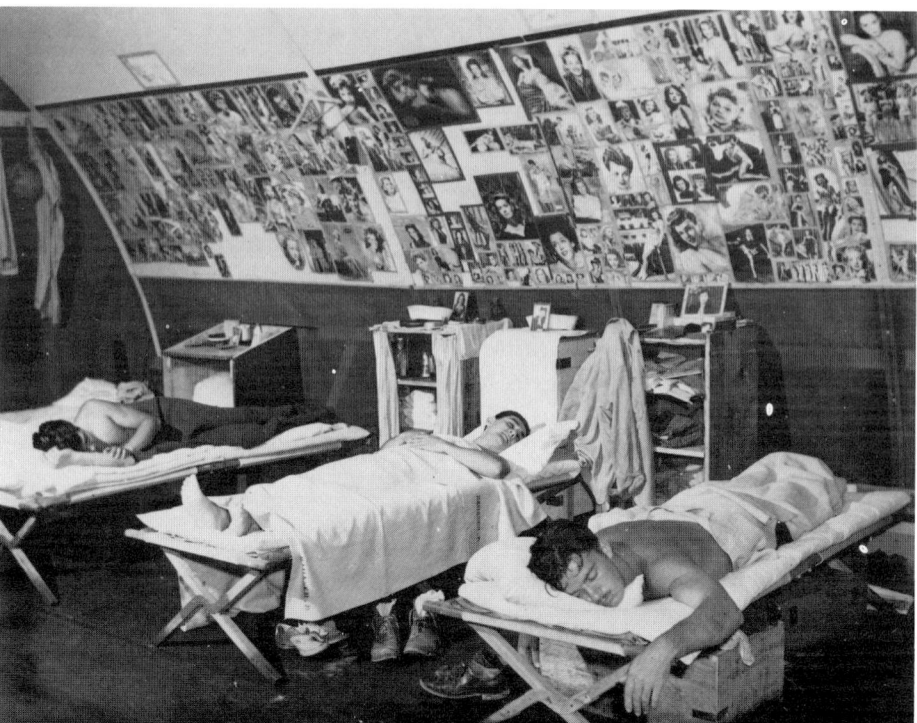

Chapter Nine • GOING HOME: Back in the U.S. of A.

The war left many servicemen with memories of dramas more intense than any they would likely encounter later in life. A sailor scrambles onto a flaming fighter to assist the trapped pilot after a crash on the *Enterprise*.

them almost 24 hours to reach Los Angeles. McKinley arrived in the city at 5:30 A.M., and no trolley ran at that hour to Venice where his parents lived. Standing on a sidewalk, McKinley saw a taxi. He counted his money. Not much. Certainly not enough for taxi fare all the way out to Venice. But when the driver saw the torpedo insignia and submarine classification on McKinley's uniform, he took the young sailor home anyway.

It was still early in the morning when McKinley stepped up to the front door of his parents' home. He had not called or written to tell them he was back in the States. He knocked on the door. Then he rang the bell. His mother had been staying with a sick friend several blocks away. Through the glass panel in the door, McKinley could see his still sleepy father come to the door grumbling. "O.K., O.K., take it easy," he said as he unlocked the door and headed back toward the bedroom. He had thought it was his wife returning from her overnight

During the war, sailors honed skills that would be useful to them when they once again wore civilian clothes. Many also got an invaluable psychological boost—they were winners. And they learned that through unity, sacrifice, and old-fashioned hard work, an implacable enemy could be vanquished.

After the war, many veterans prospered. Several, including Dwight Eisenhower, John Kennedy, Gerald Ford, and George Bush, became Presidents of the United States.

PT-boat commander John F. Kennedy.

The jumper on the left is Gerald Ford, playing basketball in the forward elevator of his carrier.

visit, not his son returning from war. Then he stopped in joy and disbelief when he heard his son's voice. McKinley's mother was telephoned and told to hurry home. The family spent a few happy hours together, but only a few. McKinley called a girl he had known, only to discover that she was married. Then he had to begin the long return trip to San Francisco.

Home Country

Eventually, McKinley was issued orders and train tickets. There were five other sailors in McKinley's group. All were about 20 years old or younger except a machinist mate first class who at age 28 was called "Pappy" by the other sailors. They were all going east and everywhere they went their connecting

Like this reflection of the battleship *North Carolina*, our memories lose clarity in the rippling waters of time. But for World War II sailors who fought there, recollections of Pearl Harbor, Guadalcanal, Normandy, or Leyte Gulf remain sharp and vivid.

trains had either just left or were behind schedule. But McKinley and his mates were in no rush to end what was becoming an extended and very enjoyable holiday. Girls whistled at the sailors as they walked along the streets of Denver and Salt Lake City. When the train stopped in North Platte, Nebraska, early one morning, a crowd of women and girls were on hand to offer cakes, pies, cookies, candy bars, coffee, and sandwiches. Later, McKinley read in a newspaper that every train carrying servicemen received a similar reception in North Platte. The nation was united as never before.

In North Platte and in every small town and city, people wanted to win the war and bring the boys home. It was the same everywhere. People planted victory gardens. They shuffled food ration coupons. Women went to work in factories or on farms and even ferried combat planes from North America to the British

Chapter Nine • GOING HOME: Back in the U.S. of A.

Old Glory flies above a carrier steaming toward victory in America's Navy War.

Isles. Others filled a host of non-combat roles in the military to free men to fight. Yachts were pressed into service to hunt for submarines. Coastwalkers patrolled the beaches. Volunteer plane spotters watched the skies around the clock. Wardens patrolled streets from dusk to dawn to ensure that no lights showed from businesses and homes. Adults and children practiced air raid drills. Gun emplacements were set up in coastal cities. People kept on the lookout for spies, and there were posters everywhere reminding citizens that "Loose Lips Sink Ships."

This was the country McKinley and his mates saw as they traveled eastward. The young sailors were just as fervent as anyone else about winning the war, but after nearly three years of fighting they felt entitled to a break. Their train arrived in Chicago twelve hours late. They had missed their connection. At the ticket office they were told it would be a few days before they could get another Pullman. Here it was, a golden opportunity for play. The helpful ticket agent said a chair car was available. "No way!" said the sailors. They would wait for the Pullman and its sleeping berths.

Chicago was a serviceman's city. There were free places to stay, free public transportation, free movies—and girls. McKinley and his mates took in everything the city had to offer before they finally boarded their next train. It brought them to Cincinnati where they met more girls.

Finally, it was onto another train—the Norfolk Navy Yard and Navy discipline were waiting. But temptation intervened. Pappy had not been home in ten years. His parents lived on a farm outside Slatey Fork, West Virginia. Surely a brief detour wouldn't hurt anything. The sailors got off the train at a stop near the farm and it was early morning when they arrived. It was cold. Food wasn't rationed on farms—and neither was hospitality—and the homecoming sailors were treated to a huge breakfast. Then they slept peacefully in soft feather beds until early afternoon, relaxed and happy to be home in the U.S. of A.